VICTORIA BECKER

A Way in the Wilderness

First published by Victoria Becker 2020

Unless otherwise noted, all Scripture references in this book are taken from the English Standard Version, copyright © 2001 by Crossway, Inc. Used by permission. All rights reserved.

The stories in this book reflect the author's recollection of events. Some names, locations, and identifying characteristics have been changed to protect the privacy of those depicted. Dialogue has been re-created from memory.

The information in this book is true and complete to the best of the author's knowledge. Any recommendations are made without guarantee on the part of the author. The information in this book is not medical advice and should not be treated as such. Do not substitute this information for the advice of a licensed professional counselor. Please consult a trained mental health professional for your specific situation and needs.

First edition

ISBN: 978-0-578-75851-0

Cover art by Blake Vilven
Editing by Sarah Hayhurst

This book was professionally typeset on Reedsy.
Find out more at reedsy.com

To my incredible, dream-supporting parents.
Dad and Mom, there are no words to adequately honor you.
Thank you for believing in this book long before I ever did.
I love you both so much.

Contents

Introduction

"My life just . . . doesn't look exactly like I thought it would," I said into my phone.

A long moment of silence followed. The shock settled in. I had just uttered the thoughts that had been trapped inside of my head for months.

I thought some things would be different by now . . .

I hoped for change and I feel stagnant . . .

I'm tired of waiting and wondering . . .

Is this really all that life has to offer?

A unique blend of freedom and heaviness came over me as I realized the gravity of my words. Hearing that statement come out of my own mouth was a shocking awakening. I'd been living in an illusion for so long. My life didn't actually look like I thought it would, but I swore I'd never admit it.

For the first time in my young adulthood, I was truly honest about my disappointment. I'd said what I'd always been too afraid to admit: my life wasn't unfolding according to my plan. The process of growing up felt so much messier than everything I'd seen in movies and on social media. My words hung in the air—equal parts painful and relieving.

Somewhere along the way, I adopted the belief that suppressing my true feelings was the same as not having them. I was afraid of being ungrateful or overwhelming someone else with my brokenness, so I plastered on a fake smile and ignored my internal groans. From the outside I appeared content and cheerful. But I secretly wished some parts of my life were different. Yet even in my discomfort and disappointment, I felt shameful about wanting more.

Wasn't this just an opportunity to learn patience and stop being so self-centered? By material standards, I've got a great life . . . shouldn't I just be grateful? Am I just being dramatic?

I anxiously awaited a response from my friend on the other end of the phone with questions dancing around my mind. I prayed my honesty wouldn't change the way she thought of me. For someone who often suppressed her true emotions, this vulnerability was difficult. It felt like I was damaging my positive reputation because I'd finally chosen to be real. I didn't want to admit my hardship, but the smiling mask I always wore was now suffocating me. Hiding my emotions felt much safer than being honest, but I needed to breathe again.

* * *

At the beginning of my college experience, I lived tethered to the opinions of others, the fear of being a liability, and the limits of black and white thinking. I forced myself to feel "contentment" as a way of hiding from disappointment. I believed peace was mine to manufacture.

I was so wrong.

I used to live a limiting, unsustainable life. I used to tell my heart it was happy even when it wasn't. I crammed my schedule full of resume-building obligations, depriving myself of rest and quiet. I'd take care of everyone else before I even thought about how I was truly feeling. It worked for a while, but this lifestyle is not what we are created for. Trust me: I know. I lived this way for nineteen years, and I've got the scars to show for it.

My old lifestyle allowed me to look put together and productive, but my stomach was always turning with anxiety. I knew something needed to change, but I wasn't sure what. As much as my patterns hurt me, the fear of the unknown stopped me from trying anything new. So, I stuck to what was comfortable: stressing and striving and suppressing.

I used to believe that if I was "happy," I was lovable and worthy. I took all feelings as fact, allowing my emotions to dictate my self-worth. When my true disappointment seeped through my facade, I saw myself as undeserving and unbearable. Because of this, I never let anyone in on the challenging parts of my life. I wore a fake smile around others, but the moment I was alone I'd often break down in tears. There were too many nights I found myself crying alone in my car, coming to terms with heaps of dissatisfaction that I refused to accept earlier. I'd feel resentful toward the people I had helped and overwhelmed by the schedule I had selected for myself.

I didn't know how to break the cycle, so I found ways to cope. I became addicted to the approval of others and I pursued perfection instead of dealing with my insecurity and loneliness. And, I cried in my car at least weekly.

I think this lifestyle is common, especially in college women. We are trained to face rejections, letdowns, and changes with a brave face. Then, we're supposed to laugh it off, dance it off, or drink it off and pretend it never happened. We're told to go and go and go until we can't anymore. This is just how life is: rise and repeat.

I lived my freshman year of college this way just fine. But when my tendencies caught up with me sophomore year, I could no longer sustain the cycle. I fell into the depths of depression, sobbing in public places and withdrawing from the people who were trying to help me. I had created a life far from sustainable. It was a life that left me anxious, isolated, and depressed.

And so, when I finally said, "My life just doesn't look exactly like I thought it would," something changed in me. It was the first time I was truly honest about my emotions. It was uncomfortable and scary, but it was true. I could not let my secret feelings rule me any longer. I could not keep sugar-coating my life.

When I admitted that my reality didn't match up with my expectations, I switched direction. I stopped the cycle of stressing and striving and suppressing, if only for a brief moment. I finally allowed myself to ponder the possibility of a better life. That phone call was the first time I let someone else in on my pain, but it was also the first time I let *myself* in on my own pain. As liberating as it is to be vulnerable with others, we must come to terms with our own emotions, too. How can we process our feelings productively if we neglect to even admit their existence?

For the first part college experience, I wasn't honest with myself. I pushed away negative emotions because I didn't think I was strong enough to survive sadness. I denied my disappointment and forced my satisfaction. I believed joy would come only when my circumstances were perfect.

If I've learned anything over the past few years, it's that lying to myself never helps anyone. When I finally admitted, "My life just doesn't look exactly like I thought it would," I realized the lie I'd been living. I was faking feelings and expecting real results, all the while wondering why I felt so disconnected from my own heart. I was depriving myself of authenticity and connection. My lies had finally caught up to me.

As I said those words, I instantly wondered if others had felt the same way. In the silence after my statement, I felt overwhelmingly confident that I wasn't alone. I think we're all in the battle of living lives that don't meet all of our expectations—few realities sync up with our ideal timelines and fantasies. But we don't talk about this over vanilla lattes or post about it on social media. We are taught to only roll the highlight reels of life. So, we silence our pain and flash fake smiles. We feel like we must justify our heartache, so we try to forget it. We worry that our burdens are too heavy for others to carry, so we bear the weight alone.

Our emotions often seem too overwhelming to confront, so we ignore the feelings we're afraid of until we no longer know what we feel.

After years of living trapped in the destabilizing practice of denying my negative emotions, I think I've finally found the keys to unlock authenticity. I've learned that being honest with ourselves is the first step toward healing. After all, how can we heal if we don't acknowledge what's hurting us? Confronting our pain should not feel selfish or shameful. It is a necessary practice for a sustainable life. By doing the hard work that healing requires, we can break free from the boxes we've locked ourselves in. We can process our emotions in a healthy manner. We can live a life that we love.

What I've learned over the past few years has slowly but surely overridden my previous beliefs. I'm nowhere near perfect, but I want to share with you what I know about life so far in hopes of reminding you that you are not alone. Despite what curated Instagram feeds may tell us, life is messy. Despite the fact we're conditioned to reply, "I'm good, how are you?" when asked about our days, our emotions are much more complicated. Despite the fact we're told "college will be the best four years of your life," it is unrealistic and unwise to put that much pressure on just one chapter of young adulthood.

You're about to unfold the details of my college experience, and if I'm being honest, I'm very nervous to share my story. But I know that from it we can both grow. I want to share my story and what I've learned along the way, through the highs and lows of life, not for my glory but for your benefit. I hope this book reminds you that we are all more alike than we may believe. I pray that this story shines light on the experience of so many women, including you.

This is a story about confidence and comparison, delight and disappointment, revelation and redemption. I'm going to share my experiences with self-discovery, mental health, and emotional wellness in college, not because I want to tell you about me, but because I hope you find something in it that resonates with you. I pray that my words help you to build a pathway to your own future of flourishing. I hope that you can take some of what you learn in this book and use it to encourage someone else.

I know that being human can feel like you're lost in an endless wilderness with no direction or escape route. But I also know from experience that there's a way for you. I believe there's a path of healing and wholeness available to us all, but we have to be willing to walk through the unknown.

While you're walking toward healing, it is *absolutely okay* to admit when your life doesn't look like you thought it would. There is so much fullness to be found when you get honest with yourself. Because, oftentimes, when we get honest about our disappointments, we realize we're living a story better and more beautiful than we ever could have dreamed up on our own.

Take this book as your opportunity to learn from my mistakes. Search for parts of your own story in mine. Let it guide you as you find true purpose and peace. Keep taking tiny steps forward toward healing. Whatever you do, just don't stop walking.

I

Part One: The Wilderness

"See, I am doing a new thing! Now it springs up; do you not perceive it? I am making a way in the wilderness and streams in the wasteland." Isaiah 43:19

1

Sophomore Slump

About halfway through my freshman year of college, I started hearing about something called the "sophomore slump." I heard about the slump in the context of schoolwork or a second wave of homesickness. I heard how challenging it could be to return to school after a summer at home. There were warnings about changing friendships, overcommitment, and obligations. Whatever this sophomore slump felt like, I wanted absolutely no part of it.

Still, other students told me that sophomore year was the best of their college experiences. They told me I'd make my best friends, I'd enjoy starting major-specific classes, and I'd finally feel comfortable at school. Before I even began my sophomore year, I was simultaneously warned of the slump and told the whole thing was a hoax. Who was I supposed to believe?

From my naive, freshman point of view, my sophomore friends certainly didn't seem to be in a slump. My sophomore friends looked like they had their relationships, career goals, and campus involvements in order. It was as if the title "sophomore" came with a magic wand to magically poof all problems away. I looked at their lives through rose-colored glasses, and I wondered if I would achieve this same level of sophomore perfection.

I don't believe every single college sophomore experiences a slump. Nothing in life is ever as perfect as freshman Victoria assumed, but that doesn't mean the sophomore slump is inevitable. Everyone's interpretation of sophomore year is real and valid. But, for me personally, my unrealistic expectations for sophomore year pushed me into a lonely, dark slump. I believe that wherever you're at, with your sophomore year on the horizon or far back in the rearview mirror, this story is a call for you to examine your expectations.

* * *

Oftentimes, the sophomore slump comes as a result of the crash back down to reality after the high of freshman year. Without the hum of first-year excitement, sophomores often have more time to second-guess themselves. And, for a professional second-guesser like myself, this spelled trouble. As I settled into my sophomore status, free from the adrenaline buzz of freshman year, I began to question myself: *Am I really confident in my major? Did I find the right friends? Am I "making the most" of my college experience?*

My freshman year had been far from easy. Homesickness and insecurity marked my everyday life. I spent my first year of college constantly counting down the days until my next trip home and critiquing my body in front of my full-length mirror. I acted a bit shyer than I did in high school, nervous about how I'd be perceived. I was frequently frazzled—ask me about the time I sold back a rented textbook—and always uncertain. *Do I belong at this school? Do my new friends actually like me? Does my family miss me?*

But in the midst of my freshman struggles, I gave myself the gift of extraordinary grace. I somehow made allowances for one year of mess ups because it was my first try at a whole new world. I forgave myself for the time I woke up ten minutes before my statistics final, lost my debit card, or locked myself out of my dorm room. I excused the awkwardness of adjusting because, *No one has an effortless, easy freshman year, right?* In fact, there are books, podcasts, and people that told me freshman year was always difficult. But sophomore year? I had never heard anything about that, so I assumed perfection. Long before I finished freshman year, I began to shape my unrealistic predictions for life as a sophomore.

I remember the dreamy expectations I held so tightly as I drove my jam-packed Honda Accord from Colorado to Texas for the start of sophomore year. Nestled between boxes of sorority T-shirts and light pink room decor was a false sense of security. I assumed that once I arrived in Texas, my freshman homesickness and insecurity would fade. It was as if my summer at home had erased all my memories of college difficulties; I didn't anticipate a single setback. I entered sophomore year expecting ideal friendships, grades, and experiences.

I thought sophomore year would give me the friend group, boyfriend, and sorority experience I spent all summer dreaming about. I expected my plans to happen smoothly and according to schedule. I thought I'd be included and invited and accepted, always. I expected perfection. With a year of college experience behind me, I assumed nothing could trip me up on my second go-around. I ignored the important factors of living in a brand-new environment, taking more challenging classes, and adjusting back to college life after spending the summer months at home.

Just a few weeks into my sophomore year, my life began to stray from my perfect plan. My initial confidence faded as I received low quiz grades, struggled to find a compatible sorority little sister, and missed my family back home in Colorado. I didn't meet a cute boy to take as my date to the first formal, and I didn't feel equipped to give advice to my new freshmen friends. I was still making silly "freshman" mistakes—losing my school ID card, procrastinating on assignments, and mixing up my schedule. I felt like I could never get it right. I lived my life to the soundtrack of internal criticism: *shouldn't you know how to do this by now, Victoria?*

It seemed that when I moved into the sorority house, I unpacked a relentlessly unsatisfied inner voice along with my favorite books and beauty products. I replaced my freshman year grace with harsh self-criticism. In my mind, second chances were not an option. Struggle and failure were for freshman year only. The dysfunction of sophomore year felt like my fault because I believed the lie that I was the one in control. If my situation wasn't flawless, I thought it was a reflection of my flawed efforts.

When my sophomore year didn't live up to my far-fetched expectations, I felt like a failure. Enter: sophomore slump.

To make things worse, I constantly compared myself and my sophomore year to others. I looked at everyone else's "perfect" sophomore years through the filtered lens of social media, measuring their public successes against my private failure. I made up long, unsubstantiated mental narratives about how easy my friends' lives were, and I felt like I was lagging behind everyone else in an imaginary race. I stopped looking forward to the future because I assumed it would be a letdown. I scrolled and assumed and scrolled and assumed until I found myself discontent and isolated.

The combination of my high expectations and constant comparison led to a lurking feeling of failure. I couldn't complete *my* "perfect plan" for my life, so I lived in constant defeat. Back then I believed that I could only be satisfied once all my expectations were met. I wouldn't settle until my actual life matched my ideal. I was looking for happiness in all the wrong places.

I used to think that an ideal life was the source of true confidence. I assumed that if others saw outward perfection, their admiration would make me more certain of myself. I was prideful and confident in my ability to control my sophomore year—but only as a coverup for my insecurities and people-pleasing tendencies.

My first few months of sophomore year were certainly sprinkled with happy moments, but those moments were not enough to soothe my insecure heart. I was so frustrated at myself because the transition into sophomore year was more difficult than I'd planned for. The awkwardness of freshman year didn't instantly fade. The campus organizations I'd been so excited to join last year were now stressing me out. I doubted the strength of my friendships and struggled to balance a busy schedule. I looked in the mirror and didn't like what I saw. *Did I even learn anything freshman year?*

Through it all I never let anyone else in on my struggle. I thought I was responsible for having all the answers, now that I was a sophomore. I convinced myself that my difficulties were unworthy of anyone's attention or advice, so I put on a brave face and continued my attempt to live out my sophomore year dreams. But deep down, I was tired of my reality feeling so far off from my forecast. I was discontent, anxious, and disappointed. I became bitter; if life didn't look and feel exactly as I'd planned, I didn't want it.

I spent the beginning of my sophomore year attempting to manipulate my circumstances to match my plans. I thought I knew what I needed when, really, I was chasing after the wrong things. I laid awake at night, wondering what I could do by my own strength to change my circumstances. After only a few weeks of this pattern, my unrealistic standards sent me spiraling into a fight for my mental health.

I can now see how unhealthy and illogical these expectations were. I thought I could have my perfect life just because I wanted it, and when things didn't go as planned, I denied the pain of my reality. I was insatiable and unsatisfied. I put all my hope in a new school year instead of realizing how little control was actually mine for the taking.

Before sophomore year had even started, I had set myself up to crash. My mindset and patterns were not serving me.

This was long before I ever considered a way of life outside of comparison and ignored disappointments and forced contentment. When I look back on this time, I worry that my expectations for perfection prevented me from seeing the beauty in the beginning of my sophomore year. I wonder how many moments of gratitude and introspection I missed out on. Although that dark season is slowly fading from my memory, I'm afraid I'll enter a similar place if I'm not careful about my assumptions.

Each new season of transition, whether in college or further along, gives us a powerful opportunity to examine our trust. *Do you feel the need to micromanage every part of your plans? Or do you trust that your future is taken care of?* I think it's alright to have goals, but they must be wrapped in grace. We must admit that our ways are not always the right ways. We must stop comparing our "behind the scenes" meltdowns to someone else's front-page moments. We must learn to write our timelines in pencil.

My sophomore slump taught me about the wild power of our expectations. I started the year expecting the unattainable, and it left me disappointed. I guess I could have expected the worst and ended up "pleasantly surprised," but that feels pessimistic. I don't think either of those expectations are healthy.

I've learned that it's best if we search for a middle ground—a sort of surrender. A place where we can simultaneously admit our needs and our wants. A place where we can recognize our expectations without letting them rule our perception of the here and now. A place where we can live eyes-open to the blessings before us while still expecting a brighter future. No matter what experiences you've had with expectations in the past, I believe you have the power to move forward into a better future.

We must learn to write our timelines in pencil

Because we receive the gift of a renewing, restoring, fresh chance each day, we can heal from the hurt our expectations have caused us. Surrender changes everything. Surrendering shifts our focus away from our own lives and increases our capacity to serve others. It is the freedom from striving. It is the belief that the world does not revolve around our needs and our timing. Surrendering builds our humility, patience, flexibility, and trust. Surrender is the pathway toward healing. We can surrender our expectations. We can live free from self-criticism and shame.

Today, two years after my sophomore slump, I've tasted and seen the freedom that is available for those who fight to take hold of it. I know that life is meant to feel purposeful and enjoyable, even if it doesn't look how I thought it would. I know this kind of freedom is available for you, too. I don't want you to live with the harsh, "all or nothing" mentality I used to let drive my decision making. I want you to walk in the peace that comes with knowing you are not in complete control.

I started my sophomore year the furthest from surrender that I could possibly be. I let my expectations control me and comparison define me. I missed life's goodness because I was too busy searching for impossible perfection. I was disillusioned and defeated. I lived trapped in that cycle of expectations, comparison, and discontentment for far too long. The pattern stole my joy and sent me slumping.

But eventually, I learned to stop the hamster-wheel cycle of expectations. Once my surroundings stopped spinning, I was able to begin the process of healing. I now know that there is much more to life than comparison and control. I know the power of my expectations and the value of my emotions. And I know that you can stop the cycle, too. The healing of surrender is available for us all.

The quality of your life depends on how tightly you hold your expectations. There is a path to freedom, even in the middle of the wilderness. It's time for you to find yours.

2

Garden

Of all the things I expected out of sophomore year, depression was at the very bottom of my list. Actually, it wasn't even on my list. I was a generally happy person, and my college life seemed too "good" to warrant depression. After all, I was attending my dream school. I loved my sorority and my major. I had a great relationship with my family and big ambitions for my future. I prioritized my faith and my health. I journaled and read inspiring nonfiction books. Someone like me would never fall victim to depression, right?

I started sophomore year prepared for my insecurity to magically melt away. I expected to meet new people and to make spontaneous, sparkly memories that I could post all over social media. I expected an unrelenting sense of belonging and a newfound confidence. I never prepared for anything other than perfection and ease. It turns out that was all just wishful thinking. Back then, I had no idea what was coming for me—the unforeseen sadness that would steal my joy for months.

The first few weeks of my sophomore year turned out to be just . . . average. I expected relationships, parties, popularity, A+ grades, and a lower number on the scale to satisfy the unrelenting desire within me. But these things never gave me what I wanted. I was living a good life, but it was never good enough for me. I was hungry for a sustainable, long-term joy, but I was looking in all the wrong places.

I was more concerned with having the "perfect" sophomore year handed to me than I was with learning or maturing. I didn't realize that life will inevitably fail to meet our impossible expectations. Back then, I didn't know how to believe in myself, so I believed in the possibility of a perfect life. I dreamed up situations so unattainable that I was bound to be disappointed.

Although my surroundings changed from freshman to sophomore year, my heart stayed the exact same. Under forced smiles I was still the insecure girl I'd been my freshman year. I was still driven by fear and the need to be liked. I still wasn't in touch with my emotions or honest about my expectations. The only thing that really changed was my college classification.

Even that change didn't heal me. The title of "sophomore" just brought more pressure than I'd prepared for. I crammed my days full of the things that I thought I *should* be doing to appear impressive. Instead of making time for personal reflection or self-care, I focused on how to please other people and build my resume. I sacrificed my own needs and obsessed over the opinions of others.

From the outside, I looked impressively involved, but my motivations for serving people were selfish. I stacked my schedule with opportunities to be praised. I just wanted to feel useful. I thought I could only be valued for my actions instead of for who I am.

At first, I thought my new responsibilities would build my character. I continued to say "yes" when I wanted to say "no," secretly thriving off the compliments I received from others:

"You're so busy!"
"How do you do it?"
"You can do it all!"
Before I'd even been in school for a month, I was beginning to feel run-

down. I found myself drifting off in class, catching colds more often, and wanting to be alone. But I never saw these changes as "warning signs." I just called myself "weak" and continued to push through. No matter how exhausted, defeated, or unsatisfied I felt, I held onto my high expectations. Whenever I was overwhelmed or disappointed, I suppressed my emotions and instead dug deeper into my well of false confidence. I refused to let go of my picture-perfect plan for sophomore year.

My outside demeanor told the story of a thriving college girl. My social media posts made it look like my life was perfect, and the more times I posted, the closer I came to believing that. In conversations I glossed over hardship and overemphasized the few aspects of my life that were going according to my plan. But inside, my heart was loaded with unmet expectations and weighed down by constant comparison. My emotional wellbeing couldn't be more different than the image I promoted.

I thought that if I didn't acknowledge my struggles, they didn't exist. And if my hardships didn't exist, I'd be less of a burden to others. And if I was less of a burden to others, maybe they would love me more. And if I was loved, I could be confident. Maybe if I'd opened up about these expectations, I wouldn't have fallen as fast or as far down as I did. From this disconnect and denial came my most recent battle with mental health—this time surfacing as depression.

I ignorantly used to believe that I'm the type of person who could never be depressed. I thought depression was reserved for the more pessimistic, reflective type. That wasn't me—I could be bubbly, fun, social, and optimistic. I thought these traits protected me from depression, but they may have actually predisposed me to my sadness. I used to believe that depression was an excuse for laziness and moping around. I associated depression with negative people who were unwilling to change, and that wasn't me.

But as I learned, there is a kind of sadness that a positive outlook can't cheer up. There is a seemingly uncontrollable darkness that comes for some of us. There is a life where you don't want to get out of bed in the morning. I never asked for this life. I didn't want to be the person who couldn't get out of bed. The label of "depressed" didn't match my positive, peppy reputation. But just because I didn't acknowledge my depression doesn't mean it wasn't growing within me. My depression made its home amongst the darkness I didn't dare admit to anyone, even myself.

At first my depression disguised itself as a little "slump." I'd heard this would happen sophomore year, and while I was reluctant to admit my struggle, I knew I could survive a few unfortunate weeks. Since I was afraid of appearing weak, I didn't tell anyone about my sadness. But despite my best efforts to wrangle it in, the depression began to spread. Against my will, my melancholy tainted every area of my life, leaving me with no choice but to contact a counselor. We'll get to that part of the story later.

No matter what your personality, depression has the ability to latch onto your core fears and desires. It doesn't matter how externally jovial, social, or energetic you are if your insides are out of alignment. Depression is not picky about a person to inhabit. It looks for the falsely expectant, emotionally out-of-touch individual, and it settles in. It thrives on insecurities, past hurts, and selfish motives. Depression takes root deep inside the unsuspecting heart, and seemingly overnight, the seed has stretched into a thick, cumbersome vine, twisting itself around its victim's heart and mind and lungs and hands and soul. Suddenly, you're bound by the very thing that stemmed from within you.

* * *

If life is an exquisite garden, filled with plants that have been carefully tended over many months, then depression is a ravenous, nasty weed.

Imagine that you're a gardener, obsessed with the health of your plants. Suppose that one day an unassuming green sprout pops up in the soil, looking totally harmless. You don't recognize this plant, so you call it a weed and toss it over your shoulder. From the surface it looks like the problem is fixed. All you can see are your tomatoes, parsley, and tulips, and they're flourishing. But deep where you cannot see, the root of the weed is crawling through the dirt, wrapping its grimy tentacles around the same plants that are blooming above the surface. The root is choking the very life you've toiled to grow.

This is how depression starts. You may detect an unfamiliar nuisance in your life, like a loss of appetite, difficulty falling asleep, or disinterest in things that once made you happy. This new change is annoying but not quite alarming. If you've never experienced depression before, you'll probably assume the best. You'll probably pluck the weed and toss it behind you, leaving the roots to grow beneath the surface.

You've got some time before the weed comes back. You learn to cope. You figure out how to live with the symptom you're experiencing; your plants continue to grow despite the weeds underground. Everything seems fine. Until it isn't.

Weeks or months or maybe even years later, you notice your plants don't seem as lively as usual. You realize your life doesn't feel as brilliant and compelling as it used to feel. You wonder if something has changed, but you convince yourself that the difference is all in your head, so you don't tell others or worry about it. By this point, you've forgotten all about that pesky weed from a while back. You convince yourself that you must be crazy; your plants and your life look fine from your perspective.

You only remember the tiny weed when suddenly, hundreds of dangerous little shoots burst through the soil. You watch in terror

15

as the tendrils twist around your precious greenery—the zucchinis you were going to bake into bread or the daisies you planned to bundle into a bouquet. All these plants you had great plans for are now at the mercy of a relentless weed. Your plants are fighting to survive.

I hope that comparing depression to a weed is a helpful visual to keep in the back of your mind as I tell this story. For me, it all started with anxiety. Over the first few weeks of sophomore year, I noticed an unsettling sensation in my stomach, loads of nervous energy, and difficulty thinking about one task at a time. Little weeds.

My mind was constantly racing, so I found some new ways to release the anxiety: going on runs, making lists, or taking deep breaths. I pulled the weeds. I moved on. But my surface-level fixes could not sustain my busy lifestyle. I blinked and it was September, and I was having panic attacks almost every day; I laid awake for hours every night; I fell out of love with the life I'd created for myself. The weeds grew too big for me to manage.

Back to our garden analogy. When you see the weeds in your garden, you're paralyzed. You know you should do something, but every choice feels wrong. You're afraid to rip out the weeds because, what if you uproot your beautiful plants along with them? You can't douse the garden in weed killer because you'll destroy your harvest. You don't have enough time to pluck every individual weed, and how could you ensure you pulled out each root? You panic. You must do something . . . and soon.

People are starting to comment on how unruly your garden has become. Your friends check in on you. "Don't worry, just a rough patch," you say. Things will be back to normal soon. You shoo away observers, even wise friends who have had these same weeds in their gardens before. They lovingly dole out tips to stop the weeds from spreading, but you refuse to listen. You think you have to pull the weeds out alone, one by one, but you don't have the time.

In the first month of my sophomore year, I found a harmless looking weed in the garden of my life—just a little bud of unmet expectations, self-criticism, and disappointment. I tossed the sprout over my shoulder and continued trudging along in my comparison-filled, people-pleasing ways. I didn't realize that, just four weeks into the school year, the roots of depression had already spread vastly underneath the soil of my life. The weeds were grabbing hold of areas I couldn't yet see, but would soon feel.

By the second month of sophomore year, the sprout had burgeoned into a viscous, overwhelming weed. The weed had taken root in my disappointments without me even knowing. I watched helplessly as the weed suffocated every carefully pruned plot. My garden, filled with the fruit of my commitments, was overtaken by the snarls of depression. Relationships, schoolwork, leadership responsibilities, health, faith, future plans. . . it seemed that every square inch of my life's soil was touched by the sadness. Depression's goal is to make you complacent. It wants you to believe that the weeds in your garden are actually roses. But the weeds just continued to suffocate me while I made every effort to deny their existence.

At first I could shush the lies depression was telling me. I had tasted the sweetness of life enough times before to know that this wasn't it. I tried my best to prune the weeds away from my precious plants, but they grew back faster than I could trim them. My surface level attempts at fixing my depression ignored its true cause, and the deep roots of disappointment remained. Eventually, I gave up.

I wish that I would have shown someone my garden, because I could have uprooted my depression much quicker with a few sets of helping hands. But out of fear of seeming weak or needy, I kept my sadness to myself. My first attempts to heal my depression were not motivated by an authentic desire for health and wholeness; they were desperate efforts to protect my reputation.

you don't need to be tidy to be loved

I thought I needed to be tidy in order to be loved. I believed that if others saw me as stable, I would feel more stability. I still clung to my picture-perfect ideals, certain that a good reputation would make me feel worthy.

Back then, I didn't know that love lasts through life's highs and lows. I was so afraid of being unlovable, and I was convinced that "unlovable" and "depressed" were synonyms. I assumed everyone would leave without ever asking them to stay. But when you're with the right people, your needs are not "too much." You don't need to be tidy to be loved.

If only I could go back in time, back to my weed-ridden garden, and invite someone into my mess. If only I would have believed the truth that I was someone worth helping. If only I would have admitted to my struggle instead of filling my schedule. If only I would have known that pulling the sprouts above the surface was just a temporary solution . . . maybe then I wouldn't be writing this book.

3

Roller Coaster

Hi, my name is Black and White Thinking—you can call me B&W for short. Hang with me and you'll realize that life has only two classifications: right and wrong. Good and bad. Failure or success. For me, it's always all or nothing.

I'll enter your mind as mild discontentment. Maybe one day your essay receives a B+, and you wish you got an A. Or one friend can't come to your birthday dinner, and you wish you had a full table. Under my influence, you'll see the 89 percent as a failing grade and the empty seat at your birthday party as complete rejection. I'll tell you that if your life isn't perfect, it's a total failure. There is no in between. I'll turn your multicolored perspective into a sharp contrast between black and white.

I love to prey on insecurity—my best friends are those who don't trust their own judgment. Invite me into your relationships, job applications, and school projects, and before you know it, my filter will shade your entire life. With me your best isn't good enough, and your worst is so bad you can't possibly recover. I'll convince you that small steps of progress don't matter. I'll present you with

standards so unreachable that you must eventually stop trying.
You cannot win. I'll make you isolated and jaded; I'll convince you
that my way is the only way.

* * *

Meet "black and white thinking." Also known as "splitting" or "dichotomous thinking" or the "all-or-nothing" mentality. It's a psychology term for a mindset often associated with the diagnoses of anxiety and depression. I didn't know about the damaging effects of black and white thinking on mental health until my counselor told me about it. This mindset makes every emotion feel more intense than it really is. The black and white thinker only notices life's highest highs and the lowest lows. Everything is either awful or terrible, all or nothing—black or white. Before my counselor put a name to my thought pattern, I didn't realize that I had such a dramatic perspective.

Looking back on my sophomore year, I can spot the detrimental effects of this kind of thinking on my attitude, self confidence, and relationships. Black and white thinking only intensified the lethal combination of expectations, comparison, and self criticism that caused my sophomore slump.

The best way I know how to explain black and white thinking is as if it were a roller coaster. Imagine an endless track of sharp ups and downs, a giant metal squiggle in the sky. This roller coaster is comprised only of steep hills and sudden drops. Imagine you're riding it.

When you're at the ride's peak, it feels like life couldn't be better; you can see the panoramic views of the city and feel the warm breeze blowing through your hair. But way up there, you may be so distracted by life's momentary perfection that you forget about the next part of the track. What goes up, must come down. When your roller coaster cart shifts one degree too far forward, you'll plunge toward a dark, dingy pit below. No fun, right?

On this ride of black and white thinking, there is no time to process what happens in your life. You're only familiar with two experiences: barreling straight down, bracing yourself for the crash, or shooting up at the sky, moving so fast your bones feel heavy. The ride is missing the flat pieces of track—the ones that are parallel with the ground. These are the moments when you could take a deep breath and become reacquainted with your surroundings. But this roller coaster only offers ups and downs, exhilaration and despair. You're either experiencing the high of excessive joy or the low of dramatic depression, which both require immense energy. It's daunting and repetitive, obviously unsafe and unsustainable. But black and white thinking is the track I rode for too long. I spent my sophomore year swinging up and down those steep, unpredictable hills.

For reasons I'll never quite understand, the beginning of my sophomore year handed me one unmet expectation after another. I didn't love my life as much as I'd expected. With each letdown, big or small, I fell further into my slump. It seemed like every few weeks, as soon as I'd start to progress back into positivity, another rejection or change would send me right back to where I had started. It was a constant cycle of defeat, with each round leaving me more fragile than before.

I started my sophomore year wanting everything to be always as I thought it should. I began the year with an optimistic outlook, but that quickly changed once life didn't go as I planned. At first, I tried to convince myself that I was happy, but this failed me horribly. After a few weeks, I was exhausted and unsatisfied, and so I gave up on all attempts to regulate my emotions. I started swinging between high highs and low lows, instead of just coming to terms with my imperfect reality. I ended up in the dark, isolating valley of the black and white roller coaster.

Had I managed my expectations and been honest about my emotions, I don't think this would have happened. But I fell so far from the top that I couldn't possibly fathom climbing back up. Gravity seemed too strong; I felt too weak. I assumed the darkness would be my new normal, and so I didn't bother sharing my feelings with anyone. I thought this was just what my life was destined to feel like.

When I lived with this dogmatic mindset, I let the smallest problems ruin my days. I was constantly overthinking the normal parts of life and looking for something bad. A rushed morning, a spilled coffee, or a misinterpreted glance from a friend would send me spiraling into negativity. Even if my afternoon took a turn for the better, I would be too focused on the earlier setback to celebrate.

This pattern was problematic enough when I faced a minor inconvenience. But a serious disappointment, like a low test grade or a rejection from a campus leadership opportunity, would push me into weeks of internal darkness. Fueled by negative self talk, I would dig myself deeper and deeper into the pit discouragement. I refused to see the sunshine; I didn't believe my life could be any brighter than black.

All the while, even in my lowest moments, I refused to tell anyone about my disappointment. Even though my mind was dark and bitter, I mustered up enough strength to convince others that I was living at the top of the emotional roller coaster. I responded enthusiastically, "I'm great! How are you?" and only reported on the highlights of my day. I never told anyone when rejections hurt. I never told anyone when I was insecure. I was afraid of being "too much" for others to handle, so I downplayed my internal darkness. I focused all my efforts on others and I was praised for my positivity. But my insides couldn't be more different than my outsides.

The fall of my sophomore year is when I got stuck at the lowest point of the roller coaster. In the pit I started seeing everything as "bad" and I had no energy to process it. I simply stayed in its "badness," feeling more helpless and hopeless with each passing day in the dark. Occasionally, I would try to get the little imaginary cart back up the steep hill, but every time, gravity would pull me back down into depression. I didn't know then what I know now: I couldn't escape depression until I escaped black and white thinking. I needed to get off of this awful roller coaster.

I thought a perfect life was the source of happiness, and so when my life strayed from my dreams, I assumed everything was awful. When I hopped on the ride of black and white thinking, I unknowingly limited myself to only two emotional positions: total bliss or complete catastrophe. Black and white thinking convinced me that extreme feelings were safer than the in-between. It used to feel like freedom, but I ended up enslaved to my emotions.

I thought I was only strong enough to handle a happy, easy life that went according to my plan. I didn't trust myself to endure pain, so I tried my hardest to ensure that I never felt it. When my life was going "perfectly," I was just one inconvenience away from total darkness. When I hit rock bottom, I was convinced I'd never make it back up to the light. In either position—the roller coaster high or low, I was dependent on things I couldn't control. The up and down swing exhausted me until settled at the bottom, stuck in the depths of depression, held down by my unmet expectations.

When I reflect back on my black and white mindset, I realize just how much damage it did to me during my sophomore year. My perspective allowed me to choose between flawless, unreasonable happiness or overwhelming defeat and self-pity. It caused me to deny the majority of my emotions in a weak attempt to solve the complicated puzzle of my feelings. I limited myself to black and white when, in reality, life is a dazzling rainbow.

* * *

24

you must learn to see the world as it really is

I wish I could go back in time and tell my sophomore self that the black and white methodology is too simple. Few moments are totally successful or sad. I wish I knew back then that black and white thinking is only a temporary solution to the lifelong wrestling match with ambiguity. Let's face it: most of life is pretty ambiguous. Certainty is pretty rare. Ambiguity is the vibrant gradient of emotions between optimism and despair. The spectrum is so much greater than just black and white—every color, every emotion deserves to be recognized.

When we dwindle down the spectrum of emotions to simply black and white, we make shallow what was designed to run so deep. We limit our capability to experience the wholeness of being human. Life offers us many gifts that cannot be named, only felt. But the inability to classify emotions doesn't mean that they don't matter. Ambiguity is okay. It is necessary and inevitable. Our in-between feelings are valuable, even if they're hard to name.

Black and white thinking will never give you true peace. Once you realize this, you can begin the process of breaking free from its confines. To beat black and white thinking, you need to let yourself see the gray. You must learn to rest in the unknown. You must realize the roller coaster is lying to you; life isn't composed of only extremes. When you feel yourself at the peak or the pit of the roller coaster, it's time to change your perspective. You must zoom out of the situation and see the roller coaster for what it is: a violent, egregious cycle of emotional exhaustion.

The process is long and difficult. Your progress may feel small and insignificant at first. But someday, you will see the world in all its glorious color once again. You will inch yourself along a new, level track by the power of realistic self-talk. You must change the immoderate thoughts that once pushed you from highs to lows. You must see the world as it really is: ambiguous and messy and incomplete and beautiful.

Black and white thinking sounds like, *I just had a hard conversation with a friend and I messed everything up and she hates me now. I have no friends because of course I am not lovable, this is the worst day ever and I should probably just transfer schools and start over.*

But a moderate frame of mind says, *That conversation was difficult but it was productive. I'm proud that I spoke up for myself. I'm not sure exactly what my friend is thinking, but if she has a problem with me, she will say something. Until she brings it up, I refuse to worry about it.*

It takes practice to saturate our black and white thinking with color, but the hard work is worth it. You do not have to know all of the answers. Not everything in life needs a category. Even if your instincts first lean toward extremes, remember: you are in control of your own mind. I didn't understand it as a sophomore, but I know now—I do not have to succumb to the whiplash of my thoughts. I do not have to ride that roller coaster. It is okay to let things "be."

We weren't made to live breathless and afraid on a dangerous roller coaster. We were made to ride the level path of moderation, acceptance, and peace. As we learn to live life on a safer track, we will look at the world more realistically. We will be honest with ourselves and our people. We will learn to accept the world in all of its beautiful ambiguity.

4

A Note from a Stranger

I stared at the plastic lid of a single-use coffee cup. The oblong hole was surrounded by a halo of leftover latte. I nervously tapped my fingers on the edge of the wooden table as anxious thoughts bounced around in my mind; my worries rang louder than the coffee shop's bustling melody.

Not here. I can't cry here, I thought to myself.

I nervously surveyed the coffee shop, checking to see if I knew anyone nearby. My heartbeat thumped, and my eyes darted around the room. Thankfully, I didn't recognize the people around me. But I wondered what everyone was thinking . . . *did they notice my anxious behavior?*

I shifted my gaze back down toward the coffee cup and forcefully swallowed the lump in my throat. I tried to take a deep breath, but my heartbeat only quickened, my chest only tightened. My mind was racing faster than I could keep up with. My brain spun with a jumble of information: the text messages awaiting my response, the essay due tomorrow, the way my thighs looked in the mirror this morning, the confusing comment made by a friend the day before. . . my overstimulated head felt like it could explode. My body didn't know any way to process emotions other than to cry.

The coffee shop environment became suddenly overwhelming. I needed to be alone. I longed to cry in the privacy of my bedroom or my car, but both places were far on the other side of campus. In the afternoon hour between a class and a meeting, I didn't have time to walk there and back. I was trapped, tied down by private thoughts in the midst of very public surroundings.

Victoria, do not cry here. No one can see you cry.

It was Wednesday at 3 o'clock in the afternoon. I'd come to the on-campus coffee shop to finish up some homework before a busy evening. After an early morning spin class motivated by my negative body image, a morning full of classes I spent multitasking on my computer, and lunch with a group of people I tried constantly to impress, I was exhausted. I hadn't taken a moment to assess my feelings that day until I was sitting at the table with a textbook open in front of me. The rapid pace of my sophomore year schedule wiped out all my time for healthy self-awareness. During that season of life, I was too out of touch with my emotions to realize when a breakdown was on the horizon. And that Wednesday afternoon, a breakdown was inevitable.

I'd been feeling "off" for the past few days, but I just thought it was normal college stress and sleep deprivation. So, I disregarded my anxiety and attempted to resume my homework. I stared intently at the textbook, struggling to focus on the words through my burning eyes. I let out a shaky exhale, and my vision blurred with the tears that had been trapped inside of my body for weeks. The hot liquid glazed my eyes—two salty teardrops landed on the textbook page with a dull thump.

My tears set off a chain reaction of panic throughout my whole body. The internal name-calling began: *you're weak, you're dramatic, you're pathetic.* I couldn't let anyone see me this fragile. My best idea was to make a break for the coffee shop bathroom.

Of course, my chair screeched loudly as I pushed it back behind me to stand. I was certain that all eyes were staring at me. I put my head down and beelined toward the privacy of the bathroom.

I spent the fall of my sophomore year striving for an impossibly idealistic life. I didn't want to be someone who experienced sadness, anger, disappointment, or pain. I thought tears were an indicator of my incompetence. With the filter of black and white thinking shading my perspective, a stressful day took me instantly to the pit of my emotional rollercoaster. After a whole semester of stressful days, I was bound to break.

As I entered the single-stall bathroom, I had no choice but to look at myself in the massive mirror above the sink. I made eye contact with glassy, wet eyes. My whole body seemed to be drawn inward, tied up in knots of worry and self-doubt. I analyzed at my reflection with disgust:

> *You're weak. Crying in public, really? Stop it, Victoria. You're the problem. No wonder your sophomore year isn't going as planned. Everyone out there is wondering where you are. Everyone in the coffee shop is talking about you. They're probably telling their friends about the crazy girl crying a few tables away. I mean really, what kind of person breaks down in public like that?*

I splashed some cool water on my throbbing cheeks. Even if I stopped my tears from flowing, my inflamed face would tell the story of my weakness. I looked at my watch; I had to leave for a meeting in thirty minutes. I had to pull myself together, or else I'd have to explain myself.

> *Victoria, stop crying. Nothing even happened. You have a good life. You go to your dream school. Time to get over it.*

I snapped back into reality: I couldn't stay in the bathroom forever. I had homework to finish, and it was irresponsible to leave my things unattended for too long. I took a deep breath and decided I'd go back to my table. But as my trembling hand reached for the door handle, I began to cry again. Now the coffee shop felt like the most dangerous place in the world. Anywhere outside of this bathroom was too vicious for my tender heart. I needed absolute privacy. I couldn't let anyone see me this way, broken and emotional and defeated and human. I couldn't inflict damage upon my own reputation.

Then, I heard the sound I'd been praying not to hear: a knock at the door.

"Hello? Is anyone in there?"

I mustered up my best attempt at a calm response—"Yes, just a moment. Sorry!"—and washed my hands before heading toward the door again. With a sharp inhale, I unlocked the door and stared down at my feet as I walked back to my table. I didn't dare make eye contact with anyone around me.

I sat down and assessed the tears on my textbook page once again. The two puddles reminded me of my inadequacy, which made me want to cry all over again. I wiped my eyes, picked up my phone, and dialed my mom's number. Her familiar voice had calmed me down countless times before—surely, she could help me now. I needed her to tell me I was okay, since I couldn't convince myself.

I walked outside of the coffee shop and listened to the phone ring, praying my mom would pick up. I paced alongside a busy road, occasionally glancing at my table through the coffee shop's massive window, nervous for my unattended belongings. I didn't expect to be outside long. My plan was to talk to my mom for a few minutes, regain my composure, and return to the coffee shop like nothing had ever happened.

On the last ring, my mom finally answered. I immediately over-whelmed her with an avalanche of tear-tainted words: "Mom I cannot stop crying, and I don't even know why. Literally nothing happened—I'm just upset and overwhelmed . . . I'm the worst. I'm in public and everybody is looking at me and I have a meeting in twenty minutes and I can't breathe . . ."

The knot in my stomach began to unravel as my sniffles turned to sobs once again. I cried to my mom about how *I had to calm down right now so that I could finish the textbook chapter because there was a quiz tomorrow* and *I needed to get an A* and *actually I needed to get straight A's* and *I had a meeting in a few minutes* and *nothing felt cancelable* and *everything felt overwhelming.* By the time I'd explained my circumstance, my limited minutes to talk with my mom were almost through. She announced it was time for her to go to a work meeting, which sent me into another wave of panic. If I couldn't have her physical presence, I needed her voice. I felt like a little kid again, desperate for my mom to tell me this was all a bad dream.

My mom stopped my word vomit by calmly instructing me to take deep breaths. She told me she loved me and then she had to hang up. I whimpered goodbye and heard the click of a finished phone call.

I felt truly alone, even as cars full of people zoomed down the street beside me. My mom couldn't help me, and I couldn't help myself. I'd reached my breaking point, and I wasn't even sure why. I crumpled onto the ground, a soggy mess. My feelings felt too strong, I felt too weak. The weight of unmet expectations was too heavy for me to withstand. There, sitting on the concrete, I prayed that I didn't know anyone in those passing cars. I couldn't be seen like this.

I tried to take a deep breath, but the air felt thick and gooey, hard to swallow. This was not the year I planned for myself. This was not the life I showed on social media or told my friends about. This was not what I thought college would be like.

I wiped my nose on the soft cotton of my T-shirt and caught a glimpse of my watch—ten minutes until my meeting. I started hyperventilating, but the time left me no choice but to calm down. I quickly stood up, fixed my ponytail, and walked back into the coffee shop, heart racing and head throbbing. Maybe if I acted like I was okay, I'd finally feel okay. Maybe I could solve my sadness by pretending it didn't exist.

A slew of self-deprecating thoughts sloshed around in my brain as I reentered the coffee shop. I kept my head down, focusing on the laces of my dirty running shoes. I avoided looking at the people around me; I could sense their pitiful stares resting on my puffy eyes, and I didn't appreciate this sort of attention. I was convinced that everyone in the room absolutely hated me, and in that moment I hated myself, too.

I walked through the glass door and headed straight for my vacant table. As I placed my textbook in my backpack, I noticed a folded sheet of notebook paper nestled carefully into an open pocket. The paper was placed neatly and intentionally—obviously by someone other than me.

I was worried I'd unfold the paper to find a passive-aggressive message, scolding me for taking up precious table space and irresponsibly leaving my stuff unattended. Or maybe I'd read a note confirming the self-deprecating statements I'd already spoken over myself—that I was a mess, a helpless disruption. Maybe it would read, "You really should have your life together by now." Nervous and hurried, I crumpled the paper in my fist and speed-walked out of the coffee shop.

* * *

Although I made it to my meeting in time, my mind stayed stuck on the events of the past hour. I spent the meeting wondering what the people in the coffee shop were saying about the messy girl they'd seen crying earlier. I pondered what awful insult could be scrawled on the note that I had stuffed in my backpack. My mind buzzed with anxious thoughts, but I didn't shared my worries with anyone else. Even around the crowded meeting table, I felt alone, trapped in my own tired mind.

As per the usual, my meeting began with all eight members sharing the "highs" and "lows" of the day. I heard stories of passing grades and difficult exams, unexpected surprises and roommate trouble—typical college struggles and successes. I panicked as the question moved in a counterclockwise circle around the table we shared. My "low" of the day felt too dramatic to share. I didn't want to say anything that would change how I was perceived; I didn't want to seem selfish or incompetent or sad.

When asked for my "low" of the day, I confidently responded, "I can't really think of anything. Today has been great, actually." But the fading red splotches on my cheeks told a different story.

After my halfhearted attempt at a productive meeting, I could not wait any longer to open the note. A few steps outside the library, I paused and reached into my backpack to grab the wadded mystery. I nervously uncrumpled the paper to find a few gentle words in neat handwriting:

I know life can be hard. I'm sorry. Keep your head up. You are strong.

I took a sharp, shallow breath. This was not the harsh insult I was expecting. Instead, it was a tender act of kindness, a selfless move of empathy. The note from a stranger was an example of the grace I wouldn't give myself. These were the words I needed to hear.

Yet, my insides instantly turned with uncertainty. Part of me felt grateful for this stranger's good deed, but a larger part of me was embarrassed by this charity. I didn't want to be the kind of person who others needed to take care of. I wanted to be left alone; I wanted to keep others safe from my problems. But, as I've since learned, wants and needs are not always the same. What I *needed* that afternoon was a reminder of my strength. I needed someone to tell me that I could make it, and a note from a stranger did just that.

strength is not the absence of need

I stared at the paper for a few moments and pondered what to do next. I looked at the loving, loopy handwriting, and then I looked at the trashcan a few feet away. I am not proud of my choice. I tossed the note into a trashcan, as if disposing of the paper could undo what happened in the coffee shop. As the paper fluttered into the bottom of the trashcan, a false sense of confidence came over me. I thought that throwing away this act of kindness was a sign of my strength. *I don't need anyone telling me what I can do. Why would anyone think I needed their anonymous words to cheer me up?*

I used to think strength was the absence of need. I used to find my value in the fact that I didn't ask for help. But my martyrdom was really just a weak cover-up for my deep insecurity. I acted artificially confident and overly positive around people I knew, only to break down in tears when I was alone. I didn't know how to be vulnerable.

Vulnerability is a lot easier to preach about than it is to practice. If you search "vulnerability" on the internet, you'll probably find cutesy, hand-lettered quotes. But telling others about our pain is rarely pretty. Vulnerability is messy and uncomfortable and raw. When we aren't vulnerable with those who truly care about us, our pain will spill out in places we don't expect or want, like a coffee shop on a Wednesday afternoon.

After throwing away the note, I continued my evening by acting chipper, deflecting questions, and forgetting what happened in the coffee shop. I felt proud of myself for being "strong," when what I really needed was to be honest. I wouldn't be able to play this game for much longer.

Later that evening, right as I was going to bed I received a text message from a friend: "Hi. I hope you're doing okay. I saw you crying today. I just want to let you know I'm here if you need anything. Take care of yourself."

My heart rate sped up; here was another act of kindness that made my palms clammy. My acquaintance's well-intentioned message sent my head spinning. I felt exposed. I thought I'd been able to hide my breakdown, but now someone in my social circle knew. *What if she told other people?* I wondered. *What if she was worried about me? What if I see her and I have no choice but to tell the truth?*

My breakdown, my negative thoughts, my growing depression—they were all my little secrets. I felt safest as the only person who knew about my sadness. I believed that if I told someone else my true feelings, they'd see me as weak and incompetent. These were all lies that depression was telling me, but they felt like truth at the time. I didn't want to burden anyone, so I stayed silent. But, as I retreated from reality, my burdens only grew heavier.

I decided to go to bed without responding to the text message, but I couldn't relax after the day's emotional events. I spent the night tossing and turning in my sorority house bed. In my few moments of sleep, I dreamt I was all alone, carrying a massive boulder up a tall mountain. In my dream I saw myself weak and exhausted, barely able to put one foot in front of the other. I watched myself climb until I was no longer able to take another step, and finally, sweaty and tear stained, I collapsed under the weight of the boulder.

I woke up, heart racing, drenched in cold sweat. My sheets were damp and twisted around my legs. While I knew that I was not actually pinned under the weight of a boulder, my body felt crushed. The weight of my anxiety, my people-pleasing, my perfectionism, my black and white thinking...it had all become too heavy to carry alone.

I trudged to the sorority house bathroom, half-asleep but hyperventilating. I looked at myself in the mirror to see my disheveled hair, the dark circles under my eyes, and my T-shirt soaked with sweat. *Was this how others were seeing me, too?*

In that moment I realized I could not hide my depression any longer. The weight of the boulder had broken me. It was time to tell someone.

5

"All Better"

My eyes fluttered open at the first beep of my alarm clock. I instantly wished there was a way to turn back time, to squeeze in a few more hours of sleep before I had to face the menacing day in front of me. The thought of getting out of bed, stepping on the cold floor, and facing the human interaction was beyond overwhelming. Depression urged me to stay wrapped in the safety of my pale blue comforter, hidden from the possibility of vulnerability.

After fantasizing about an easy, comfortable day in bed, my sensibilities reminded me that I needed to attend class. I reluctantly rolled out of my lofted bed, walked over to my desk, and grabbed my phone. Instinctively, I checked my notifications. The first thing I saw was last night's unopened text message: "Hi. I hope you're doing okay. I saw you crying today. I just want to let you know I'm here if you need anything. Take care of yourself."

As I reread the kind words, I felt shameful instead of supported. I couldn't believe someone else knew about my weakness. I wondered if she was worried; I hadn't answered her text, even with hours to craft a reply. I considered various responses: "Thank you," "It was no big deal," or "I'm fine," but nothing felt right.

38

Was this text message a God-given opportunity for vulnerability? Or was it just an intrusion on my personal life? My anxious mind fluctuated between feelings. In a moment of panic, I pressed the button on the side of my phone to make the screen go dark. I feeling instantly safer with the message out of my sight.

I dragged my sleepy feet across the rug and reached for my Bible and journal. Then I trudged down the sorority house stairs, activating my daily routine. As I made my coffee in the stillness of the kitchen, I replayed yesterday's events in my mind. I watched my empty mug fill with fragrant caffeine as I imagined my coffee shop meltdown from an outside perspective. I pictured myself weepy and fragile, my shoulders slumped, and head down in the midst of a bustling atmosphere. I saw myself speed walk toward the bathroom, trying my best to restrain tears that were begging to break free. I remembered my trembling hands reaching for the door to exit the bathroom, only to quickly retract back in fear. I imagined what it would look like to see a nineteen-year-old college girl crumple to the ground in despair on a Wednesday afternoon. As I replayed the embarrassing memories, one thought dominated my mind: *That girl is a mess. Victoria, you're a mess.*

I grabbed my coffee and plopped down in the corner of a comfy white couch. Thankfully my self-deprecating thoughts dissolved as soon as I opened up my Bible in the quiet of the morning. While almost everything else at the start of my sophomore year had been turbulent and dissatisfying, my relationship with God felt more real than ever before. I think that's often why we go through stormy seasons—to become more dependent on God. After all, if everything in life was easy and within our control, we wouldn't need a higher power. But we can't do it on our own, and so we need a source of strength outside of ourselves.

I sighed and turned the pages of my Bible. On that particular date, I happened to be reading 2 Corinthians chapter 12. Verse 9 stopped me in my tracks: "My grace is sufficient for you, for my power is made perfect in weakness."

I paused and thought of all my weaknesses; I could list thousands. My sophomore year had been like a magnifying glass on my failures. Under the influence of my unrealistic expectations and unproductive thinking patterns, I felt very aware of all my flaws. I was clumsy and sensitive and stubborn and afraid. I was always running late, always tired, and always thinking about my never-ending to-do list. I was familiar with my weaknesses, but I never saw them as places that God could work.

The verse was highlighted in fluorescent pink and the word "perfect" was underlined in my bible. I'd read 2 Corinthians 12:9 many times before. But today it tapped into a different part of my soul. The verse was all too relevant after what had happened yesterday—I felt anything *but* perfect. I had shed tears in a coffee shop, collapsed on the sidewalk, and discarded a note from a selfless stranger. I felt weak, ashamed, and alone. But the Bible told me there was purpose in my shortcomings.

When I read 2 Corinthians 12:9 that morning, my perception of my imperfection began to change. If my weaknesses truly existed to display God's perfect power, maybe I could talk about my struggles with someone else. Amidst the serenity of the early morning, my heart began to open to the possibility of vulnerability.

As I continued reading, the second half of 2 Corinthians 12:9 caught my attention. "Therefore I will boast all the more gladly of weaknesses, so that the power of Christ may rest upon me."

I stopped reading, feeling confused once again. *Boasting* about my weaknesses? I was just barely considering sharing my weaknesses with one trusted friend. But here the Bible was instructing me to *boast* about my weakness. I didn't understand. Why on earth would I gladly tell someone about my weaknesses? Was I supposed to talk about my failures and faults like they were praiseworthy?

As a sophomore I hated talking about my shortcomings. I didn't want to be a burden to others. I believed that sharing my struggle would make me unlovable. And yet, God orchestrated my morning so that I'd read a Bible verse all about vulnerability. He brought me to 2 Corinthians 12:9 to tell me a message I couldn't deny: it was time to share my struggle.

As I finished my coffee and reading for the morning, my emotions fluctuated between trust and terror. I wanted to be obedient to the Bible. I wanted to share my weaknesses and allow God's redeeming power to shine through my struggles. But I was so afraid of what someone else might think when I talked about my hardship. *Was my sadness real or all in my head? Am I just weak? Do I really have a valid reason to feel depressed?*

I pondered the potential people whom I could tell about my degrading mental health. I imagined what words I'd say, and I wondered how a third party would respond to my pain. The possibility of someone rejecting or minimizing my depression petrified me. The thought of telling someone about my struggle was more frightening than my actual feelings. I worried that telling my truth would feel exposing rather than encouraging. *Who could I trust with such a precious secret?*

I didn't want to seem flawed or inadequate. Back then, I thought life was all about being perfect and doing things right on the first try. I wish I could go back in time and tell myself that life is inherently flawed, and humans are always going to mess up. Perfection is not our purpose.

We were created for more than fake smiles and forced contentment. We were made for honesty, connection, and vulnerability. Our most authentic life is on the other side of admitting our weaknesses. If only I could have known this before my sophomore year, I would have saved myself a lot of heartache.

* * *

41

perfection is not our purpose

As I went through the rest of my day, my mind stayed thinking about the possibilities of whom I could tell and how they would respond. By the afternoon I'd analyzed every single person I knew, and no one felt right. I convinced myself I couldn't confess to anyone. *What if they asked me questions for which I had no answers? What if they gossiped about me? What if vulnerability ruined my reputation?*

After internet searching "who to tell when you're depressed," I decided on an answer. Despite my shame, I knew that I needed to talk to someone about my struggle, and quickly. I just didn't want it to be a friend with an opinion and the ability to share it with others. I felt too breakable to risk sharing my sadness with someone in my social circle. So, based on Google's recommendation, I decided to involve an outsider: a licensed professional counselor.

I hesitantly began to type an email: "Hi, My name is Victoria Becker. I'm a sophomore at Texas Christian University, and I'm looking for a female Christian counselor because I've been really anxious lately and I think I may be depressed."

I looked over my shoulder every few minutes to ensure that no one saw the message on my laptop screen. Just the act of typing this email filled me with embarrassment. This was *not* how my sophomore year was supposed to go. I planned on being invincible, experienced, and knowledgeable this year. *Where was the confidence I started with?*

I felt like an imposter. I posted on social media about a life of confidence and ease, telling others of my success and happiness. I flashed fake smiles and humbly bragged about the ease of my life. But none of this was true. Inside I was unraveling and rotting away.

A counselor wouldn't think I was crazy, right? Surely, it was her job to help "dramatic" people like me. A counselor could keep my secret and fix my problems. I assumed I could go to counseling for a few sessions, and then I'd feel better. I wouldn't need to tell any of my friends where I was going, and I didn't think they'd really notice a change in me. I just needed to confirm or deny my depression and learn how to stop crying in public places. Back then, I didn't realize just how deep down the roots of my depression went. I reread my email to the soundtrack of my nervously thumping heart. In a brief moment of boldness, I pressed "send."

When I reflect on the choice I made with the gift of hindsight, I wish I had told someone in my real life before I told a counselor. When I sent that message, I put myself in the position of waiting for some unknown being behind a screen to reach out and help me. As I anticipated the counselor's response, I continued to live in isolation, making silent assumptions that all of my friends were thriving. My seclusion made me feel even crazier. Until the counselor responded, it was just me and my secret, dark thoughts. I wondered if she'd even reply, and I decided that maybe it wouldn't be the worst thing if she didn't.

* * *

A few days later, I was running on the treadmill at the campus rec center when the counselor called. At the sound of the ringtone, I slowed my speed to a walking pace. I picked up my phone to answer the call and paused, briefly remembering 2 Corinthians 12:9. But as I tapped the phone, an intense fear washed over me. I decided that I was not strong or confident enough to share my weaknesses with anyone, not even a counselor. I instantly regretted ever sending that email. The internal critic began. *Stop being so dramatic. You don't need help. You should be able to figure this out on your own.*

I anxiously looked over my shoulder, worried that someone could tell what I was about to do. I put the phone face down in the treadmill cup holder and let the call ring through. I listened to the voice in my head instead of the truth I knew deep down.

The phone continued to ring as I increased the speed of my treadmill, much faster than it was before. I tried to sprint away from my problems, away from the life I lived but did not love. I let the burning in my leg muscles distract me from my depression.

After thirty minutes of endorphin-boosted bliss, I picked up my phone to see a voicemail from the counselor. Even before I listened, I already guessed what I'd hear. I was sure the counselor would confirm the things I'd told myself many times before: that I needed to grow up and get over myself. I expected the voicemail to go something like:

> Hi, Victoria. Thank you so much for your inquiry about counseling, but unfortunately, I am too busy to accept any more crazy people at this time. Plus, I looked at your social media, and it looks like you're doing great. Don't you go your dream school? Don't you love your sorority and your major? You have nothing to be sad about. Please get a handle on your life and stop being so worried about everything. Bye!

Deep down, I worried that a counselor's input would confirm my worst fear—that I was unlovable. I was worried she'd tell me I was a burden. But I realized that whatever the counselor said in the voicemail, it couldn't be worse than what I'd already said to myself. I apprehensively tapped my phone screen to play the voicemail.

I brought the phone close to my ear and a soothing voice told me:

> Hi there. Thank you so much for your inquiry about counseling. I am so sorry for what you're going through. I would love to chat with you over the phone sometime in the next few days, and we can get to know each other better. Then, if you think we would be a good fit, you can come to my office for our first session. I am proud of you for reaching out because I know that is scary. I hope you are taking care of yourself. Have a good night.

45

Breathless from my workout and my fear, I began to process the words I'd just heard. Again, just like in the note from a stranger, the words were so much more kind than I anticipated. I was so used to the negative voice in my head that any outside gentleness was shocking. I didn't believe that love could be for me. *What if the counselor's sweetness was just a facade? How could I know that she didn't want to meet me just because I'd pay her?* I decided I wouldn't call the counselor back.

Later that evening, still buzzing off nerves from the voicemail, I decided that I needed to respond to the friend who'd texted me the day before. After typing and deleting and retyping a message ten times, I finally settled on a nondescript response: "Hi. Sorry it's taken me so long to get back to you. Thanks so much for reaching out. Just a bad day, but I am all better now!"

I pressed send.

"All better."

My lie was now permanent. Another missed opportunity for vulnerability.

I told my friend I was completely good, totally healthy. I said I was "all better," as if the events in the coffee shop hadn't become my everyday reality. My text told of one bad day, when in reality, it had been a bad *year* with no end in sight. I told her I was "all better," even after avoiding a counselor's call and refusing to be vulnerable with anyone, even after sobbing in a coffee shop, and even after self-diagnosing myself with depression. I was so afraid of sharing my weaknesses that I had forgotten about how God's power could be made perfect in them. I thought that if I acted like I was "all better," I would heal. I didn't realize how much hard work I'd have to do in order to feel better again.

6

Two Words

My phone buzzed, disturbing my midday study session. Before I even read the notification, I was already anxious. I hesitantly glanced down at my phone, hoping the notification wasn't from the friend who'd seen me crying in the coffee shop. A few days after I'd sent the "all better" message, she still hadn't replied. I wondered if she saw right through my last-ditch efforts at composure. I felt like she knew my text was a lie. Meanwhile, I kept trying to convince myself that my response was true. *It was just one bad day*, I thought to myself. *I'm all better now. All better.*

I felt like a fugitive on the run from vulnerability. Every time my phone lit up, I feared it was a message from that friend. I agonized over her potential responses. *What if she calls me out on my fake happiness? Does she know about my depression? What will I say if she asks me to hang out? What if she tells me I have a serious problem and should see a counselor?*

I nervously read the notification on my phone. Thankfully, the name of my friend was nowhere on the screen. *Good. She isn't worried. I'm so glad I won't have to tell her that I'm depressed,* I thought. I breathed a sigh of relief. I was safe from vulnerability—at least for now. I could continue to keep my sadness as my secret.

Instead of the text message I expected to receive, I was surprised to see the name of a different friend light up on my screen. Immediately I wondered, *What if she saw me crying, too?* Curious and fearful, I clicked on the notification to open up the message. It read, "Hey! I miss you. Wanna grab dinner soon?"

I slowly exhaled, relieved by the unassuming text. I was grateful for the invite, but soon my anxiety kicked in. *If she knew that I was struggling she would have mentioned it, right?* I wondered. The only way to find out was to go to dinner with her. I decided that a potentially awkward dinner date was better than eating alone with only my dark thoughts to keep me company. So, I sent a nonchalant reply: "Yes, I would love that! How about tonight?"

Within a few minutes she responded, "Yes! I am free. 6?"

We made plans to meet at the dining hall, and I continued on with the rest of my day. I tried not to wonder whether she knew I was struggling. I was actually excited to meet up with this friend, and I hadn't been excited for anything in a while. She was a friend who I saw often in passing, but rarely one-on-one. I wondered about her life; she had a massive grin on her face most every time I interacted with her. Her social media posts were adorable. She seemed like she had a lot of friends. *Was she having a perfect sophomore year?* I wondered.

* * *

Later that afternoon, while I was walking back to the sorority house after class, my phone rang. I anxiously glanced at the caller ID and recognized the number. It was the counselor, calling me back after a few days of silence. I had the time and privacy to talk, but I instantly decided not to pick up the phone. A conversation with a counselor would make my depression a reality. Answering the phone would force me to admit my struggle.

I couldn't imagine continuing to live life this, broken and alone, but this way was all I'd ever known. Palms sweaty and heart thumping, I placed my phone into my backpack. I quickly zipped up the backpack's open pocket, as if placing the phone out of my sight would erase the fact that a therapist had my phone number. Rather than taking the risk of vulnerability, I reverted back to what was familiar. Like I'd done so many times before, I ignored the opportunity for authenticity and I pushed my pain deeper beneath the surface.

The remaining vibrations before my phone sent the counselor to voicemail seemed to last for years. As I continued to walk, phone buzzing in my back pack, I saw an acquaintance I knew from a campus leadership organization. "Hey! You look cute today!" I stated enthusiastically.

"Thank you!" she said. "How's your year going?"

"So good," I replied. "I love being a sophomore!"

We proceeded to chat about how *great* everything was going until my phone finally stopped vibrating. I knew I wasn't being honest, but I assumed she definitely was. Interactions like these just enforced the narrative I'd been telling myself all year: *everyone is doing better than you are.*

For the remainder of my walk back home, I thought more about vulnerability. *Was it even worth it?* The thought of answering the phone and admitting that I needed professional help was too overwhelming for me to process. I was angry at myself for reaching out to a counselor in the first place. *Why did I share my struggle? I wasn't ready. It wasn't worth it.*

Factually, I knew that I needed help. But my heart was so afraid of what might happen once I admitted my weaknesses. I believed that once I said the dreaded words—"I need help"—out loud, my dreams of a perfect college experience would shatter like a dropped china plate. I didn't want to risk cutting myself on the jagged edges of what would be left behind.

Just a few steps away from the sorority house, I saw a poster advertising on-campus mental health services, various hotlines and support groups. After my refusal to answer the counselor's call, my encounter with this poster felt like a cruel sign from above. I wondered if students at my college actually utilized those services. For a brief moment I considered the possibility that other students in my midst were hesitant to ask for help. I wondered if others struggled with vulnerability like I did.

I soon arrived at the air-conditioned sorority house. As I opened the door to the sanctuary of my empty bedroom, a bright orange sticky note caught my attention. I'd scrawled 2 Corinthians 12:9 on the neon slip of paper and stuck it to my bulletin board a few days ago. As I set my backpack down on the ground near my desk, I couldn't help but read:

My grace is sufficient for you, for my power is made perfect in weakness. Therefore I will boast all the more gladly of my weaknesses, so that the power of Christ may rest upon me.

I'd stuck the neon note on my bulletin board a few days before. It was a reminder that I shouldn't be ashamed of my shortcomings. The verse was supposed to be an encouragement, but instead, it made me feel like a failure. As I read those words, I remembered all of the times I'd run from vulnerability. Instead of allowing my weaknesses to be conduits of God's power, I concealed them by missing calls and crafting overly positive responses. As much as I logically understood that it would be wise to open up, I could not overcome my fear of rejection long enough to get the words out. It was like I was caught in the middle of a tug-of-war, vulnerability versus isolation. Both options felt unbearable. I didn't want to continue living in loneliness, but I was too nervous to be honest. After living the same way for my entire life, change felt impossible. Back then I didn't truly understand that God's grace was sufficient for my insufficiencies.

I looked at my clock and saw it was time to go to the dining hall to meet my friend for dinner. I grabbed my keys and headed for the door. After a ten-minute walk, I swiped my ID card to enter the dining hall and selected an empty table for us to sit.

My friend arrived soon after, and we began the awkward shuffle of selecting our food from the buffet-style setup. We settled into conversation, beginning with safe topics: summer jobs, new classes, family, and roommates. The chatter was pretty predictable and surface level, right where I felt comfortable. Just as I began to drop my guard, my friend shifted the conversation to a place I didn't particularly want to go.

She began timidly. "Victoria, can I tell you something?"

"Yes, of course!" I responded, too enthusiastic to be truly genuine. Behind my bright smile, my insides were tingling with anxiety. I had no idea which direction the conversation was about to turn.

My friend took a sharp breath and shifted in her plastic chair. "Okay, well, my year hasn't gone exactly like I planned."

I laughed nervously. Without much thought, I replied, "Me too."

In the silence after my statement, I played a mental movie of the moments that hadn't gone according to my plan for sophomore year. I remembered tears caused by the homesickness that I swore I'd be done with. I remembered the fraternity formals that came and went without me receiving an invitation. I remembered feeling worthless and empty and ugly and inferior. I remembered the friendships that weren't fulfilling me, all the times I said "I'm fine" when I really needed help, all the moments I felt rejected and alone. My trip down memory lane brought all of the exhaustion and disappointment from the last six weeks bubbling to the surface. My depression felt like it was crawling out of my heart and wriggling around my body. I convinced myself that my friend could see my struggle right through my skin.

"Really?" she responded, equally shocked and curious. With a nervous laugh, she added, "Okay, wow, good. I had no idea you felt the same."

I realized it was too late for me to steer the conversation in a different direction. I tried to keep my response unemotional and blasé, all the while praying I could change the topic.

"Yeah, I mean, I had high expectations for this year, and I just . . ." My throat tightened before I could get any further. *Was this my moment to be vulnerable?*

A million arguments against vulnerability cycled through my mind. The haunting internal dialogue began at once. *Victoria, you barely know this girl. She knows your other friends. . . what if she tells them your secret? What if this is all a setup to expose your weakness?* My thought spiral made me feel as if the dining hall walls were closing in on me. I was now trapped at this table, seated across from someone who had seen too much of my weakness in a single statement. I could not say more.

I realized I had stopped talking mid-sentence, and so I quickly saved myself by saying, "I'll be right back. I have to go to the bathroom."

I promptly stood and walked away from the table. With a pounding heart and tight chest, I pushed open the bathroom door, only to see my reflection in a full-length mirror. I stared myself down, critiquing every inch of my body. My eyes were dark and sunken from sleepless nights. My shirt was wrinkled from my nervous grabbing at the fabric. The healthy glow I'd flaunted at the start of the year was now long gone. I looked like all the life had left my body. I didn't recognize myself.

Alone in the bathroom, the fluorescent lights highlighting my flaws, I leaned forward and gripped onto the sink to stabilize myself. Even the simple act of standing up straight felt debilitating in the moment.

How did I get here? What have I gotten myself into?

There were no answers, only a tornado of questions demolishing my already shaky confidence.

My eyes filled with tears. I didn't want to go back out there. *How could I possibly face the friend who I'd just begun to share my heart with?* I thought through every possible scenario and response, certain the dinner would end in disaster. I wanted to feel known, but I didn't want to tell someone my struggle. I wanted fulfilling, deep friendship, but I couldn't risk my reputation. I rinsed my hands in freezing cold water, attempting to feel something other than anxiety. In my weakness I whispered, "God, help."

In the midst of my trembling, a tiny spark of courage miraculously caught flame in my heart. It was an ember of boldness I can't explain, but I know it was not produced by me. This newfound confidence was a supernatural intervention. Even as I stared at the timid, teary version of myself in the mirror, strength began to rise up in me. My emotions told me otherwise, but I felt a calling I couldn't deny. I knew it was time to share my story. Even if I only got a few words out, I knew it was what I had to do. It was time to be vulnerable, to live out 2 Corinthians 12:9 instead of just reading it. Before I could stop myself, the burst of supernatural faith carried me out the door and into the evening chaos of the dining hall.

Once my friend saw me walking toward our table, I had no choice but to continue toward her. I sat down, apologetic and awkward. As the conversation resumed, I hoped for a brief moment that my friend would switch topics to something more comfortable. But she moved the conversation back in the direction of vulnerability—this time extending an undeniable invitation for my response.

"I'm not really sure why but I just feel like I need to tell you this" she began. "Sophomore year has honestly been so hard. I don't think I'm having as much fun as everyone else. It's like freshman year all over again, but this time I'm expected to have it all figured out. To be honest, I've really been struggling with my mental health." she said, anxiously awaiting my response.

I swallowed. This opportunity for vulnerability couldn't be any more evident. I couldn't deny that God had ordained this conversation with a purpose in mind. Now it was up to me to decide whether I wanted to take hold of His plan. I did not want to be disobedient to the courage I'd received just a few minutes before. It was time for me to share.

As I looked into my friend's eyes, I felt our relationship would be forever changed by this conversation. I squeezed my hands into fists under the table, fingernails digging into my palms, and I quietly uttered two words that would change the course of my sophomore year.

"Me too."

Even though I curated a perfect life on social media, ignored calls from a counselor, and acted like I wasn't struggling, God still made a way for me to be vulnerable. It's funny how God gave me the moment to live out 2 Corinthians 12:9, even after I'd continually run from what the Bible asked me to do. God often gives us what we need, even if it's not exactly what we want. His desire for us is growth over comfort or convenience. He wants to equip us and empower us to do hard things, like admit our weakness or help a friend through theirs.

"Me too." Two simple words that changed everything. I didn't know it at the time, but there would be hundreds more moments of uncomfortable vulnerability along the path of healing. I was just getting started.

7

Castle

The rest of my dinner conversation was clunky but continuous. As it turns out, vulnerability doesn't unfold as seamlessly as seen on TV. But even in the awkwardness, there were moments so effortless that I swore I was talking to myself. While I entered the dinner date distant, I left feeling deeply connected to this friend. That's the power of healthy vulnerability: it changes the trajectory of relationships in an instant. One honest moment is more unifying than a thousand surface-level interactions. Vulnerability bonds and heals and strengthens like nothing else in this world.

When I heard her story, I began to realize that not everyone else's lives are as perfect as they say or post on social media. This conversation was the start of a long journey of learning that everyone is dealing with something behind the scenes. It was an unbelievable relief for me to know that someone in my direct proximity was struggling similarly. I left that raw, unguarded dining hall conversation with a greater confidence.

My moment of vulnerability was terrifying, but I survived. Before I had this conversation, I didn't know that I could be brave and scared at the same time. Like most fears, once I actually did the thing and lived to tell the story, I found a new strength within me. I didn't realize my own power until I was forced to get uncomfortable.

I didn't share the full extent of my depression with this friend right away, but we planned on grabbing coffee the next week to update each other on how we were doing. I walked away from that dining hall dinner table feeling lighter, as if my heart was flesh again instead of stone.

* * *

It would be a few more days before I responded to the counselor's call. Despite the progress I made during that dining hall conversation, my path to authentic vulnerability was far from perfect. I was not automatically ready to talk with a counselor just because I had one honest conversation with a friend. I still feared what a counselor would say about my worries or problems.

I really hate to admit this, but this book is about vulnerability, so I must tell you: there was one more time that the counselor called me and I pretended not to notice, sending her to voicemail. *I know, I know.* I wish I just had answered the dang call, too. But healing is a long and winding road. We cannot expect excellence overnight.

In the counselor's third voicemail, she gently asked if I was still interested in her services and requested for me to call her back. I worried that if I did not respond to this message, I wouldn't hear from her again. If that were the case, I would have to start this process all over again with someone new. I didn't want to tell *yet another* person about the depression that was so hard for me to articulate. So, motivated mostly by the desire for less people to know about my condition, I finally mustered up the courage to call the counselor. In the security of an empty sorority house early in the morning, I nervously dialed her number. I listened to the ringing and prayed she wouldn't answer. It would be so much easier to leave a message rather than to talk with a real live human.

Ring. Ring. Ring. "Hello."

The same voice I'd heard on the voicemail three times was now echoing in my ear. The counselor was no longer a faraway figure but an actual, tangible person. She knew my struggle, and she was ready to discuss it with me. I froze, unsure of what to say.

"Hi, this is Victoria. I, um, emailed you a few days ago . . ."

Before I could spend any more time awkwardly explaining my situation or feverishly apologizing for all of the missed calls, the counselor took control of the conversation. She didn't expect me to come with a script or talking points; she just needed me to be myself. My counselor knew long before I did—counseling is meant to be a place of healing, not a place of performance.

I paced around the sorority house study room, frantically looking at the door to ensure no one would enter. Even though I knew there was a slim chance I'd encounter anyone else at this early morning hour, I still feared that I'd be walked in on, found out, and laughed at. *How could I possibly survive if my secret got out?*

The counselor began to ask me gentle questions about how I felt, who I was, and how I got here. I didn't provide her with the clearest answers. The cloud of my depression was so dark and thick that I could hardly see behind or ahead of my current emotional position. This was long before I realized the harm my high expectations had caused me. It was almost impossible for me to imagine a future without this kind of pain.

The counselor told me a bit about herself and gave me an opportunity to ask questions as well. Our thirty-minute phone call went by quickly. At the end of the call, the counselor invited me to meet her in person. I was nervous, but I figured that I'd made it too far to turn back now.

We decided on a Tuesday afternoon, and with a click the damage was done—I was officially going to counseling.

A few more emotion-filled days later, it was time to meet the counselor in person. I timidly snuck out of the sorority house and I was grateful I didn't run into any friends along the way. I wondered what I would have told them if they asked where I was going. Back then, I didn't understand that going to counseling should not be cause for shame. Just as we go to a doctor if we're struggling with our physical health, we should visit a counselor when we're struggling with our mental health. And just like we aren't expected to share our in-depth medical history with everyone we meet, we shouldn't have to spill all the details of our counseling sessions to strangers. But we'd tell a friend if we had a doctor's appointment, and so we should feel free to briefly mention the fact that we're in counseling. The only way to break the stigma is by saying something.

On Tuesday afternoon I drove to the counselor's office, feeling uneasy. *What questions would the counselor ask? How would I answer?* My hands were tightly clenched on the steering wheel, knuckles turning white. I blasted my favorite worship music in hopes of distracting myself from the overwhelming sense of my impending doom. But the music was of no use; there was no volume loud enough to override the haunting thoughts in my head.

I kept my foot on the gas, fighting the urge to go back home. I realized that, while I could have made a "wrong turn" or "forgotten" the appointment, it would be of no use to me. If I missed my appointment, I was the only one who would truly suffer. I would return to campus having made no progress, just out the cost of one counseling session. Fifty-five minutes of excruciating vulnerability lie in front of me—vulnerability that I'd voluntarily signed up and paid for. I had no clue how I was supposed to survive almost an hour of explaining my sadness to a stranger. But I was so desperate to escape my depression that I kept on driving toward the counselor's office, praying my risk would in some way reward me.

In another instance of supernatural boldness, I arrived at the building, parked my car, and walked in. I shifted nervously in the red leather chair, observing the waiting room as the clock counted down to counseling time. The counselor's office really wasn't much different than any other doctor's office, which made me feel a bit better about being there. Maybe I wasn't as crazy as I felt.

After a few minutes, the counselor walked confidently out of her office and into the waiting room. I nervously followed her down the hallway, forcing chatter about the weather until she reached her designated space. She closed the door behind me, and I settled into a chair directly facing hers. After a few minutes of inevitably uncomfortable introductions, the counselor's tender questions began to flow.

I started the session attempting to wear a brave face. I kept my answers blunt and generic. I told the counselor that my life wasn't too difficult, and I just needed someone to listen to a few of my problems. She smiled knowingly and asked me about various areas of the college life I'd built for myself. We discussed my friendships, family relationships, classes, and commitments. I intentionally emphasized the brightest, most beautiful parts of my life while downplaying the gray that had recently shaded my schedule. I exaggerated my happiness, hoping the counselor would believe the same story I'd been telling myself over and over.

"I live a good life really. I'm usually pretty happy. I think that I'm just stressed. Honestly, I've been crying a lot, but I'm not really sure why. I'm probably just tired. I have a really busy schedule. I'm good though," I explained nervously.

I looked at the counselor, analyzing the subtle shifts in her face to see if she believed my story. The corners of her mouth remained parallel with the ground. Her loving eyes continued to stare into mine. It felt as if her gaze was not at me but into my soul, like she had a special ability to see my most secret parts.

After what seemed like an eternity of awkward shifting in my seat, she finally broke the silence. "Can I ask you a question?"

I nodded.

She paused, contemplating how to properly arrange her words for the greatest impact. Gently, she said, "I know you have a good life. You don't have to justify that to me. I just want to ask . . . if you're so happy with your life, then why did you come to counseling?"

I blinked. That question shook my soul awake like an alarm clock. I realized my facade was not foolproof. I finally understood the limits of my lies. The counselor saw right through my forced smile and fake optimism. I wondered if anyone else saw past my positive disguise, too.

I so badly wanted my sophomore year to meet the far-fetched expectations I'd unpacked when I moved in. But a few months in, it was clear that my sophomore year was going awry. I was sad and sleep deprived. I was anxious and insecure. I put my worth in the opinions of others. I was obsessed with my reputation. I struggled to believe in God's plan for my life. This was not the college experience I'd pictured, but nothing would change until I admitted it.

I had convinced myself that I could still salvage my year by at least *appearing* content. While I wasn't exactly happy with my life, I didn't want others to know about my disappointment. I wanted to be strong and easy to be around, so I denied the parts of me that I thought were unlovable. But it was time for me to come to terms with my disappointment instead of hiding it behind texts that claimed I was "all better" and notes crumpled in trash cans. I had to be honest.

When I started going to counseling, I thought that I could nurse my miserable heart back to health in private, one session at a time. I hoped that I could maintain a flawless exterior outside of the counselor's office.

I didn't expect the process to be messy or difficult. I didn't anticipate the challenge and change I'd experience. I didn't want anyone to know

I was growing. But I've since learned that you can't put on a show and heal at the same time. Life is about more than your image. Life is about inviting the right people in to your mess. You need help to uproot your never-ending weeds. You cannot do this alone.

In order to face your deepest dirt, you must completely surrender to the process of recovery, a turning over of old soil. You cannot pretend your garden is full of flowers when the growth is really weeds. You must address the weeds one by one, or they'll choke the few flowers you have left. Counseling was my first attempt at weed-pulling, and let me tell you: the journey was far from easy or clean.

* * *

I was used to pretending that my life was perfect and refusing to let anyone see my true condition. I didn't even want a counselor to know the extent of my brokenness. I wanted to be mysterious and admired from a distance. So, I hid from vulnerability and authenticity and connection. I isolated myself like Rapunzel locked away in a castle.

No one forced me to stay up there. In fact, friends and family often asked me to open my door and come down the stairs. They wanted me with them, not locked away up high. But I thought my castle made me powerful and beautiful and safe, so I stayed.

But then, on that Tuesday afternoon, the counselor gave the opportunity to be honest. She empowered me to unlock the tower door and peer down the stairs. It was time to reveal the real me, anxious and depressed and hurting and doubting. She cared enough to see me up close.

life is about more than your image

So, with a shaky, small voice, I responded to her question. Why *was* I going to counseling? I started to explain. I hesitantly began to tell the complicated story of my college experience, from beginning to end, sharing every letdown and embarrassment and failure. As I talked about these incidents, tears began to fall down my cheeks. After a year of suppressing my disappointment, I was finally processing my heartache.

While I cried to the counselor that Tuesday, the walls of my castle began to crumble. Each statement dismantled another brick, breaking down the fortress that was isolation disguised as protection. Thirty minutes later, the counselor's office was a metaphorical construction demolition site. Pain, loneliness, and desperation were strewn about like bricks and beams. The castle that once kept me isolated was now in pieces at our feet.

When I think back to that first Tuesday afternoon counseling session, I don't remember the exact words that the counselor or I said. I don't remember finding perfect solutions or solving problems. But I remember how I felt. I remember that the counselor stayed there through the demolition of my castle walls. She didn't mind the mess I made. She didn't need me to apologize or clean up. We just watched the castle crumble together. And from those broken pieces, she empowered me to rebuild something more beautiful.

Over the next few months, I would undergo the refining process of renouncing the lies I once had believed, examining my thought patterns, and uprooting the depression buried so deep under layers of wanting that "perfect" college experience. Each step of progress would require another nerve-wracking moment of vulnerability, another crumbling of the walls I'd built around my heart. But with every new secret unearthed, I would access more of the wonderful complexity we call living. The journey toward healing would expose me, challenge me, and confuse me, but it would be deeply worthwhile.

Get out of your castle. You aren't safe up there; you're isolated.

Unlock the doors you've kept closed for so long. Call in a counselor, a parent, or a few friends to bulldoze the walls you've built up around your heart. Experience the fullness of being known, seen, and heard.

II

Part Two: The Way

"The light shines in the darkness, and the darkness has not overcome it." John 1:5

8

Oasis

My suitcase wheels rumbled behind me, skating across frozen morning ground as I scurried toward the warmth of Denver International Airport. I quickened my pace, each step taking me closer to the airplane that would carry me far away from my worries. My family and I were headed for tropical paradise—ten days of escaping the Colorado cold and celebrating the start of a new year.

It was winter break between the first and second semester of my sophomore year. I'd returned home from school with a battered heart and emotional baggage far heavier than my suitcase. The overly confident girl who drove to Texas at the start of the year was long gone by December. That girl had been replaced with a frail shell of who she once was, cracked by her own impossible expectations and unwillingness to be vulnerable.

I was sore from the heartbreak of unfulfilled plans, but I thought some family time and a couple of Christmas cookies could fix me. I figured that I was just a few solid nights of sleep, a few heart-to-heart conversations with old friends, and a few belly-laughs with my younger sister away from full restoration. I was waiting for someone or something to save me from my sadness. I thought a trip home for the holidays would do just that.

But the first few weeks at home didn't heal me like I'd hoped. It wasn't the situations that disappointed me. My childhood bedroom felt warm and familiar, my high school friends hugged me tightly, and my favorite holiday treats tasted just as delicious as always. Home didn't let me down, but it didn't quite heal me either. I still felt the same empty longing I'd experienced at school. My stomach still twisted with anxiety every time I wondered what someone else thought of me. I still ran from vulnerability like a fugitive. I continued to scroll through social media, silently resenting the people who were living the life I thought I deserved. Home did not fix me. Instead, it pushed me further down the dangerous path of escapism, looking for something to fix the problems I was too scared to face.

Since time at home in Colorado wasn't lifting my depression, I hoped that my family's upcoming Hawaiian vacation would solve my problems before I headed back to school in January. The few days between Christmas at home and our departure for Hawaii seemed to drag on endlessly. Time was slowly slinking along as I anticipated the long-awaited escape from my depression. I hoped that the tropical trip would magically reset my thought patterns and habits because I couldn't bear the thought of enduring depression any longer. There was no way I was strong enough to survive another soul-wrenching semester slump. I needed to be "better" by the time break was over.

A little escape would surely fix me, right? I just *knew* that once I set foot on the island, I'd be free of the overthinking, the fear, and the sleepless nights of first semester. I was *convinced* that my negative thoughts would dissolve into the Pacific waves and drift far away from me. I assured myself that after my trip, I'd return to college for the second semester feeling confident and calm again.

As human beings, we are predisposed to love a good escape, like a Netflix binge, a theme park, or a romance novel. These escapes can be stress-relieving and even good for our mental health, but they don't change the reality to which we must return. As a sophomore overwhelmed by my unmet expectations, anxiety, and depression, I acquired the destructive habit of escapism.

Merriam-Webster defines escapism as the "habitual diversion of the mind to entertainment as an escape from reality or routine."[1] At school I'd created a life I hated to live. I stuffed my schedule with obligations to feel important and I tried to ensure that everyone liked me. I neglected time for self care, and I let anxiety steal my peace. *No wonder I wanted to escape!* I tried to numb my anxiety through distraction, deception, and overindulgence. I turned to Instagram, straight-A's, dark chocolate, and ultimately a vacation—desperate for a few moments of fulfillment.

I was afraid of returning to the reality of my sophomore year after winter break. I was counting on a vacation to heal me, but we can't heal by running away. Escapism is a coping mechanism, not a solution.

* * *

A few days into our Hawaii trip, the familiar symptoms of panic began to boil inside of me. As I sat adjacent to the calming blue waves, I began to feel sticky, dizzy, and scared as I had many times before. I knew by my shallow breaths and racing heart that I was about to have an anxiety attack. Usually, these attacks were triggered by a distinct outside factor, like a tough test or a tight schedule. But in Hawaii my circumstances certainly didn't warrant this emotional response. I was safe and surrounded by natural beauty. I had no obligations other than soaking up the sun and spending time with my sweet family. So, why did I feel anxious here, surrounded by the scent of hibiscus and the sound of crashing waves?

I quickly gathered my beach supplies and scurried back to the condo where we were staying. In the safety of the empty bedroom, I released my pent-up panic with an outburst of tears and hyperventilating. I thought this vacation was supposed to fix me, but it seemed I'd accidentally packed my problems in my suitcase along with my swimsuits. I guess I'd assumed my anxiety and depression would flee once I got to Hawaii. But if that were the case, how could it be that sitting on my favorite shoreline, healthy and happy and blessed, my mind was *still* racing?

When our circumstances change, whether for a ten-day vacation or an unexpected opportunity or a post-grad move to a new city, we carry our baggage with us. We can only run so fast and far until our brokenness catches up. In my case even a tropical oasis couldn't fix me like I wanted it to. In that moment I realized that my depression wasn't coming from my circumstances; it was coming from within me.

I hopped on a plane and flew to the prettiest place on earth, far from the school situations that were stressing me out. I changed locations and I was around different people. But no matter what changed around me, depression still raged inside of me. Even on the sands of Kauai, I couldn't fully relax. Even in the presence of my encouraging family, I felt insecure and insignificant. Even thousands of miles away from my busy school schedule, I was still stressing. If a trip to a tropical paradise wouldn't satisfy my deepest longings, then what could?

I reached for my phone, collapsed onto the condo's queen-sized bed, and let the tears flow. Instinctually, I started scrolling through social media to numb the pain. The posts on my screen told me that everyone was *thriving* during their winter breaks. I saw pictures of other families vacationing in places far more exotic than Hawaii. I read captions about people going after their goals. I tapped on posts of people posing with their adorable best friends and boyfriends. I wiped my eyes as I compared my island anxiety attack to everyone else's filtered moments. The voice in my head got louder and louder: *you can't possibly keep up. You'll never be good enough.*

After scrolling and sobbing some more, I came up with a brilliant idea: *what if I posted a photo to show the world how much fun I was having in Hawaii?* Maybe a well-filtered snapshot from my vacation could compete with all the other posts I'd just seen. I scrolled through my camera roll and selected a photo from a few days before, back when I was dressed in a cuter outfit and not in the midst of an anxiety attack. I used apps to adjust the photo's lighting so I looked more sun-kissed and the sunset looked more vibrant. I thought up a witty caption, added my location—"Kauai, Hawaii"—and hit the "publish" button. *Maybe if I get likes and comments on this photo, I'll feel a little better about myself,* I hoped.

My photo popped up on my social media feed, but I didn't feel much different than I did a few moments before. I refreshed the Instagram app over and over again as likes and comments rolled in. But the virtual attention only offered me momentary happiness. My post didn't fill the void in me like I had hoped it would. I still felt anxious and alone, even though my social media depicted otherwise. My vacation didn't feel picture-perfect, even though that's the story I told the internet. Posting didn't make me feel better; it just made me feel fake.

Throughout the rest of our island getaway, I remained tense and discouraged. I didn't have another anxiety attack, but the overall sense of uneasiness didn't leave me alone either. With each passing day of continued depression, I came to the realization that a vacation wasn't going to save me from my sadness. Even in the most beautiful place on earth, surrounded by my favorite people, I still wasn't satisfied. Eventually, I'd have to deal with my own darkness. The island couldn't fix my problems for me.

I had spent the first half of my sophomore year trying to manipulate my environment to my liking. I thought that once my circumstances were perfect, I would feel peace. I used to believe I'd be content and anxiety-free once my life matched all my expectations. That's why I set the bar so high for my sophomore year. I strived for perfection until it wrecked me.

My trip to Hawaii taught me that peace isn't created by circumstances—not real peace anyway. Soon enough, the ice cream will melt, the sun will set, and the buzz of endorphins or a glass of wine will wear off, and you're still left with your sadness—just you and the darkness inside of your head.

Like all of life's temporary pleasures, the moments of tropical bliss I experienced on vacation were fleeting. After every moment of "peace" I felt on the island, I quickly returned to my fear, anxiety, and depression. That's when I realized that if I didn't like my life when I was relaxing on the shores of Kauai, there was no way I'd enjoy my life anywhere else.

I didn't want to feel like I had to fly thousands of miles away from my relationships, problems, and schedule to find happiness. In Hawaii I finally realized that I couldn't keep looking for a new TV show, friendship, or number on the scale to satisfy my relentless longings. At the end of the day, I was the one stuck with my own tired heart, and I was the only one with the power to change that. I wanted to like my life again.

When even tropical paradise couldn't bring me joy, I knew that something inside of me was to blame. In Hawaii I realized that there's no escape that can provide permanent peace. I decided it was time to take healing into my own hands. And so, when I returned back to Texas for the second semester of my sophomore year, I decided it was time to take my healing seriously. I began to assess my commitments, priorities, and relationships and how they affected my overall wellbeing. I began the slow, winding journey through the wilderness, one small step at a time.

The work of rebuilding is challenging but worthwhile. Because, for lack of a better way to say this, we're stuck with ourselves. Whether you're on an island or it's just another regular weekday, you are living and breathing the benefits and consequences of your choices. No person, place, or escape can distract you forever. You've got to carry your baggage around for the rest of your life. No one else is responsible for your healing.

Something monumental happens inside of you when you finally realize the value of your own flourishing. You have the strength within you, and you just have to commit to finding it. You deserve to enjoy your life. You deserve to find freedom from expectations and assumptions. You deserve to know who you really are and how you were made to thrive. You deserve the opportunity to pursue the best version of yourself. You don't have to carry your baggage alone.

When you say "yes" to change, you must say "no" to comfort. You must release all of all the escapes and disguises you used to need to feel okay, and you must ask God to fill your empty hands once again. You must ask what you believe about yourself and the world. You must embrace the wise counsel of those who've gone before you. And then you must follow through with the painful process of uprooting. Those nasty weeds in your garden will resist your tending, but you are stronger than your weeds.

No matter what anyone has told you, even that nasty voice inside your head, you deserve a life you love to call your own. Your life has inherent, unshakable meaning and purpose, and *you* are responsible for designing an existence you can get excited about.

When you decide you are worthy of a life you love, you take back the power that anxiety, depression, and expectations once had over you. When you realize your escapism isn't serving you, you're finally able to appreciate the present moment.

you deserve
a life
you love
to call
your own

9

The "Best" Years

I returned to Texas for the second semester of my sophomore year committed to changing everything about my life. I wanted to keep all those promises I made to myself in Hawaii. I couldn't continue to live like I did during the first semester—anxious and depressed, crushed by my own expectations. I was ready to take my healing seriously and put my needs first. I was eager to create a life I loved, but I had no idea where to start.

I remember the moment I returned to my sorority house room after a month of vacancy. As soon as I opened the door, one thing was clear: my room needed a major makeover. Everything in that shoebox of sorority house space felt wrong. My room was a portal back to the overwhelming, lonely life I'd lived first semester. I looked at my bed and remembered all the nights I woke up sweat-soaked and panicky. I looked at my full-length mirror and remembered all the times I had stared into it and critiqued my body. I looked at my journal and remembered all those tear-stained pages.

I wanted to erase all of those bad memories from my mind and pretend the whole "slump" had never happened. I needed to get rid of everything and start over. So, I spent the next few days rearranging my room. I thought that switching the position of my pillows or replacing the photos on my bulletin board would reverse the damage that first semester had done to my heart.

When my room makeover didn't satisfy me like I'd hoped, I decided it was time to make more changes. I cut my hair shorter, I tried to eat healthier, and I made a conscious effort to meet new people. I wrote letters to my family in Colorado and I scheduled meetings with my professors. I deleted my social media apps and attempted to go to bed early. I bought a new journal and I went to weekly counseling. From the outside I looked like I was healing. But none of these lifestyle changes were helping me like I'd hoped. I was still depressed; I just looked different.

When you are healing from depression, editing your external life is a solid place to start. It's true that when we sleep enough, stress less, and eat healthier, we'll feel a bit better about ourselves. Our inner and outer worlds are closely connected. But it's unwise to make external changes and expect internal results, which is exactly what I did. Instead of facing my feelings, I made significant lifestyle changes. It looked productive, but I was really just avoiding the hard work of healing. My surface-level lifestyle alterations were just tiny Band-Aids on a gaping wound. I was covering up my depression, not healing it.

External efforts are healthy and helpful and good. But we get into trouble when we use external tactics to avoid sifting through the sadness inside of us. This is what I was doing at the start of second semester. I used external change as *yet another* mask to hide behind. My surface-level healing produced only surface-level results. By the end of January, I was exhausted, weepy, and guarded like I was in the fall. The whole world felt overwhelming and unmanageable once again.

But no one would ever know this because on the surface, I looked like I was healing. I was living a more positive and balanced lifestyle. I was going to weekly counseling, I was trying to spend more time with friends, and I was even training for a half marathon. My tendencies didn't match those of a stereotypical depressed person. My friends and family complimented me on the positive external changes I'd made since the fall. But they didn't know the true condition of my heart.

I wasn't sobbing in public places anymore, but I wasn't happy either. I was making more intentional choices, but I still didn't love my life. Everything felt numb, dull, and kind of pointless. I was passionless and purposeless, despite my well-kept exterior. This wasn't the life I had promised myself back in Hawaii.

* * *

I think that oftentimes mental health struggles are portrayed in the media as exaggerated, explosive storms of emotion. Before I was diagnosed with anxiety and depression, I certainly thought this way. I used to think that anxiety only meant a perpetual fear that the world was about to end. I used to believe that in order to be depressed, you had to cry all the time and live with a constant frown on your face. But that's not always the case. Take me for example: I was involved in a handful of campus organizations, exercising regularly, going to church, doing well in school, and posting smiling pictures from sorority events on social media. I had a reputation for being enthusiastic and involved. But, deep down, I was living in despair. I wasn't afraid of the end of the world, but I was afraid of rejection. Maybe I didn't "look the part," but I was struggling.

Mental illness is a wide spectrum. On one end, you can be completely derailed by your sorrow and worries, like I was during first semester. But there's another kind of mental illness that I don't believe we talk about enough. A person with anxiety and depression can appear fully "functional;" but inside they're always feeling slightly sad and scared. That's how I felt in the spring.

My first semester anxiety and depression were like a dangerous thunderstorm. It left my life damaged and in disarray. The metaphorical sun came out for a moment when I came to my realizations in Hawaii, but as soon as I returned to campus the clouds returned too. This time, my struggle wasn't a thunderstorm. It was a slow, consistent drizzle of rain from a colorless sky. This storm was not as obviously violent and damaging as the first, but it was still raining. The anxiety and depression were still there, even though the worst of the storm had blown away.

There are two specific characteristics you need to be diagnosed with depression. There is anergia, which is an abnormal lack of energy, and there is anhedonia, which is the inability to feel pleasure. When the two characteristics are significantly interfering with your daily life, a doctor may declare you as depressed. During first semester of my sophomore year, my anergia and anhedonia disrupted every aspect of my life. By the time second semester rolled around, I could manage my anergia and anhedonia a little better, but I was still exhausted and unhappy. My depression felt different, but it was still difficult. Through it all, my thoughts and actions were influenced by an underlying anxiety that never quite seemed to resolve itself.

Once an intuitive, emotional person, I'd lost all my feelings by the start of February. Life was dull and uninspiring. I thought I was stable, but I was really just numb. The days were so gray for so long that I forgot the feeling of sunshine. I lost all of my motivation to make the changes I'd promised myself back in Hawaii. There was nothing in my life that felt worthy of my limited energy.

I didn't realize all of this until I was at a Valentine's Day party in my sorority house. A few days before the actual fourteenth, a large group of sorority girls gathered in pajamas for a Valentine's celebration. The evening had most everything I loved: the color pink, cozy clothes, and music worthy of a dance circle. Yet, I wasn't excited for the celebration at all. I could only come up with reasons to be anxious about the gathering. I spent the day attempting to hype myself up about the party, but my tired heart just wasn't in it.

When the time came for the celebration, I felt nothing but the slightest tinge of dread. My heart and mind were exhausted from considering every worst-case scenario. Normally, social situations like these would pump me up. But in February I felt like an emotionless zombie, even around the people I loved. I could barely will myself to wear my fake smile. I didn't want to chit-chat with people who knew nothing of my anxiety and depression. I didn't want to laugh and dance and act like I wasn't completely drained. The party seemed like an obligation rather than an opportunity.

The moment I entered the bustling party in the sorority chapter room, I was already planning how I could make a socially acceptable exit. I looked around the room full of people I loved, feeling much more overwhelmed than excited. I feared what they thought of me. I wondered if they could see through my facade. I compared my happiness to theirs; I doubted my value. I *wished* I was enjoying the party, but that simply wasn't the case. I used to feel so comfortable in this environment, with these people, in my own skin. But that night, I felt nothing but alone in a crowded room.

Time moved in slow motion. I convinced myself to stay at the party for just one more song, one more conversation, one more cookie—but eventually, I couldn't take it any longer. The exhaustion of my depression hit me at full force. I'd spent the party comparing and criticizing myself instead of connecting with others. I had to leave, or I would crumble right there in the middle of the dance floor.

Over loud music I shouted something to my friends about needing to leave. I slithered out of the dance circle toward the safety of my room on the second floor. With tears welling up in my eyes, I walked up the stairs toward the safety of my bedroom. *You're supposed to be having fun,*

I thought. *You're supposed to be making lifelong memories. You're supposed to be happy. Victoria, what is wrong with you?*

Everyone else who lived on the second floor was downstairs at the party. As I walked down the empty hallway, I simultaneously shamed myself for not socializing downstairs and embraced the quiet solitude of the vacant second floor. It was only in isolation, free from the opinions of other people, that I could breathe. Since I was alone, I didn't have to worry about my reputation or hide my feelings.

My depression lied to me and told me that isolation was the only way to feel peace. But I wasn't really winning, and this wasn't real peace. I was just a slave to my sadness, following the marching orders of depression.

* * *

I woke up the next morning drained and depleted. I laid in bed and scrolled though photos of myself from the night before. The snapshots of my smiling face told a very different story than the reality of my night—I wondered what I'd have to do in order to feel as happy as I looked in pictures.

In the midst of my morning scrolling, an email notification popped up on my screen—it the university post office telling me that I'd just received a letter. I wasn't expecting any sort of mail, but something about this letter felt urgent. Something deep inside of me knew that I needed to read the letter that morning. I left the sorority house a few minutes early and stopped at the post office before class.

As I made my way through the morning air, I reflected on the previous night's party. At the time it had felt too overwhelming to stay downstairs. But now, I was a little bummed that I'd missed out on the remainder of the event. I couldn't be content. I didn't trust my own decisions. I wondered what people thought about my early exit, which sent me into yet another spiral of anxiety.

I realized that my circumstances weren't fulfilling me, and neither were those small lifestyle tweaks I'd made at the start of spring semester. I was going to counseling, sure, but I dreaded every session. I felt isolated, yet I wanted to be alone. Nothing in my life had really changed since last semester. Healing wasn't happening on my timeline.

I needed a reminder that I could make it through this. I needed to see a way in the wilderness, just a tiny glimpse of light. And thankfully, in the stillness of the campus commons on a Friday morning, I received just what I needed to fuel me for the long road ahead.

The post office employee handed me a standard white envelope. As soon as I saw the familiar curve of my own handwriting on the front, I knew exactly what was inside.

> *Dear Victoria,*
>
> *Today is August 30, 2017. I am writing this as part of a sorority new member education meeting. I am still adjusting to the heat here in TX, but I like it. I'm pretty confident I made the right choice to come to TCU. I definitely miss my family though, and I wonder if my homesickness will go away soon? My biggest struggles are self-confidence, taking time to rest, and body image. I hope you will use this time in college to "find yourself" and overcome your struggles. Whenever you read this letter, I hope you're still being your authentic self and smiling often.*
>
> *Don't forget that these are the best years of your life.*
> *Love, Victoria*

I blinked, stunned by the words of my freshman self. I remembered exactly where I'd written this letter to myself: sitting on the floor of the sorority chapter room, the same room where the party had taken place last night. I had no idea when this letter was going to be mailed back to me. Actually, I thought it was supposed to come back when I was a senior. It seemed too early, but the letter came at just the right time.

So much had changed since I wrote that letter; and yet, so much had stayed the same. To be honest, my freshman year expectations weren't much different than the ones I started my sophomore year with. I wanted perfection, ease, popularity, and attention. I never thought I'd end up like this—anxious, depressed, and unsure of what to do about it. This was not the college experience I'd planned for.

One line from the letter stood out to me: "Don't forget that these are the best years of your life." I read the letter over and over, lost in my thoughts. Was this the best my life would ever be? If that were the case, then college was incredibly disappointing. Who's to say that life must reach a peak and then decline? I knew there had to be more to life than this.

As I read that statement I'd so naively written to myself as a freshman, I finally felt the power of my expectations. I came to college believing the societal cliché: "these will be the best years of your life." I wanted all the fun of college and none of the hardship. I wanted to grow up without ever having to change. I wanted college to be this perfect place that would fix my problems for me and prepare me for the "real world." But no place can heal your brokenness for you. Before I even began my college experience, I had set myself up for failure because I expected the impossible.

Our predictions for the future can damage our perception of the present. When things don't look like we thought they would, we can automatically discount the goodness right in front of us. When we get obsessed with perfection, we miss out on what God planned for us all along. I don't know about you, but I don't want to miss out.

We cannot hold ourselves back any longer

What if we took the pressure off of ourselves to make college the "best" years of our lives? What freedom would we find if we stopped putting labels on large spans of time? What if we as a society were more honest with ourselves and each other about life's highs and lows?

I think it's time we rewrite the narrative. We cannot hold ourselves back like this any longer—our assumptions and expectations are too powerful. We must stop setting ourselves up to feel defeated.

No more "best" years.

10

Buds

Let's go back to our garden analogy. It's rare to see a single flower blooming all alone in the midst of dirt. If not surrounded by other flowers, the bloom is often crawling through the thick of other greenery. Flowers flourish in bunches, and I believe humans are like that, too. Try as we may, we cannot thrive all alone. We were designed to grow alongside others—*buds*, if you will.

Back when I was a sophomore, I didn't really understand the power of friendship. Sure, I had friends, but I didn't know the depth of connection I was worthy of. I ran from vulnerability because I thought solitude would make me more strong or admirable. I was absolutely unwilling to ask for any sort of help. In group projects, in leadership positions, in the daily grind of college life, I would *never* utter my needs. I wanted to be a hero instead of a friend.

I was afraid of being selfish, so I made myself small. Instead of admitting my needs, I focused solely on others. Most all of my relationships were one sided: I would give and give and never allow myself to take. I would listen and listen and never allow myself to speak my truth. I would love and love and never accept affection in return. I thought I was being a martyr, but I was only serving so that I could hear the words "thank you" and feel important for a fleeting moment. Every time I minimized my needs, I was actually missing opportunities to make genuine connections with others.

All humans have needs, even those who claim otherwise (like I used to). After years of living as a martyr, my needs eventually roared so loudly that I could not ignore them. My resentment from a lifetime of pent-up desires eventually bubbled to the surface, overflowing in the form of anxiety attacks, endless tears, and eventually, a depression diagnosis. I didn't know it at the time, but my heart was crying for the community. I needed people who I could be real with. This battle was too big to win on my own.

I'd spent the first year and a half of college building an armor around myself. I wore this thick, clanky armor everywhere I went. The metaphorical metal was so opaque that no one could possibly see through to my true self, needy and imperfect. I worried that if I ever took the armor off and exposed my emotional bruises, my friends would instantly leave me alone with my problems. But true friends want to see all of you, both your shiny parts and rusty old junk. Performance is for stages, not friendships.

While going to counseling certainly helped me to grow in vulnerability, I never practiced it outside of the counselor's office. I didn't tell anyone how I truly felt, not even God. Despite my counselor's promptings to share my honest feelings with family and friends, I stubbornly continued to wear the heavy armor draped over my shoulders.

I returned to school for the spring semester believing that I could heal in a way that wouldn't inconvenience anyone else. Some of my friends knew about my mental health struggles, but I never told them how I was doing day-to-day. Whenever they'd ask how I was doing, I'd insist I was fine. I wanted them to believe I'd learned to manage my anxiety and depression. But my secrets weren't protecting me; they were weighing me down. I thought I was doing the "right" thing, but the inauthenticity was exhausting. I didn't realize that my vulnerability would *bless* others way more than it would burden them.

So, I continued to put up a forced, joyful front with others. I wore the armor around even my closest friends. It wasn't that I never shared any details about my life; I just chose only to share very specific, calculated parts that I felt comfortable exposing. For example, I'd gladly be "vulnerable" when discussing difficult college classes, but I'd never share the truth about my negative self image or what I was learning in counseling. I was picking and choosing vulnerability in a way that only benefited me, myself, and I.

My depression told me to keep the door to my heart locked and the windows to my life closed, and I listened. I convinced myself that my friends would stop loving me if they saw inside my brain. I felt like I had no story worth sharing. So, I let my introverted tendencies lead me into isolation. I didn't have to be painfully honest *or* fake happy when I was alone. For this reason, loneliness felt like safety, even if it came at the high cost of fading friendships.

I imagine it would be frustrating to be a friend of mine back in that season. The trust imbalance between my friends and I was so clear; getting authenticity out of me was almost impossible. Deep down, this felt wrong, but I didn't know any other way of relating to people at the time. I wasn't sure how to tell my friends that I was struggling, so I stayed silent.

Despite my best efforts to conceal my struggles, my truest friends could see right through my armor. Even as I turned increasingly inward, they'd continue to pursue our friendship. In the rare time we spent together, they would gently ask me for more details when I told them I was "good." These people affirmed my baby steps of vulnerability without making me feel like they were trying to "fix" me. I am so grateful for their flexibility and patience. If you have a friend like this, tell them how much they mean to you. If you don't have this friend, then be this friend.

Eventually, after feeling a lack of connection in my relationships and receiving loads of encouragement from my counselor, I decided that it was time for a change. I could not keep isolating myself, pretending I did not have needs because I was afraid of being a burden. I could not keep wearing my armor. I could not keep acting healthy and whole when my heart felt the opposite. I didn't know how to do it, but I realized it was time to tell my people how I'd *really* been feeling. No more castle, no more armor: just my honest-to-goodness self and my honest-to-goodness struggle.

Sharing the ins and outs of my mental health struggles with my friends was the absolute *last* thing I wanted to do. I remember rehearsing for the revealing conversations days in advance. I would write down phrases on sticky notes and practice being vulnerable in front of the mirror. I'd practically memorize the words of vulnerability, only to chicken out when the time came to speak. Instead of being brave, I'd revert back to my bad habit of glamorizing my life. I'd leave the conversation feeling defeated. *Why couldn't I change?*

What I've since learned, is that we cannot muster enough strength to change on our own. Think about it: if that were the case, you would have probably done it by now! Maybe we can self-motivate for a week or a month, but our own resources will eventually fail us. If I had enough strength to get out of my depression alone, believe me, I would've chosen that route.

Here's where I think I went wrong: I was telling myself the same narrative and expecting different results. I entered into my vulnerable conversations believing that my feelings weren't valid and my friends didn't care about me—*of course* I didn't feel confident enough to tell them about my depression! Change is impossible when we stay stuck in the same pattern.

My depression lied to me, my fear of rejection haunted me, and my insecurities convinced me to stay isolated. But we were made for more than loneliness. Human beings are here to lean on and learn from one another. We need to borrow the strength and faith of others when we don't have enough of it on our own. We were made to bond, we are worthy of belonging. We need a source of hope outside of ourselves.

I couldn't fully heal until I asked someone for help. I'd have to let people in on my suffering in order to grow. I certainly learned this the hard way. The only reason I finally got real with people was that I couldn't stand my loneliness any longer. And so, by the messy and imperfect process of telling the truth, I inchmealed my way along the journey of healing. I spent the next few weeks revealing my broken heart to the most important people in my life. With a shaky voice and inconsistent eye contact, I would cough up words to explain the way I was feeling. My courage came from 2 Corinthians 12:9 and that unexpected conversation I had in the dining hall.

To this day, I can vividly remember each conversation when I told a friend about my mental health struggles. I can still close my eyes and picture the look on their face, where we were sitting, the clothes I was wearing—all of it. "I am depressed" were the scariest words I've ever uttered. I thought "I am depressed" was synonymous with "I am unlovable."

Back then, I'd spend the majority of every conversation about my mental health apologizing obsessively. I would apologize for feeling sad and having needs. I'd apologize for not being stronger or more put together. I'd talk about my depression like it defined me. But anxiety, depression, or any struggle for that matter, does not define a person. It is not who I am; it is just something I deal with.

Mental health is just one singular element of our entirety. And mental health is something that *every person* must protect and regulate in one way or another. Just because someone isn't diagnosed does not mean they do not struggle occasionally.

My conversations about mental health were uncomfortable, and I was often uncertain of their impact. But I don't blame myself or my friends for a moment. There is not a "one size fits all" plan for how to navigate this wilderness. And so, I don't want to write one for you in this book, as much as I wish I could. It would be ignorant and insensitive to pretend that everyone's experience is the exact same. All I can do is tell you my story and hope that it gives you the ounce of courage that you need in order to tell the truth.

My friends responded to my story in all sorts of ways. Most were genuinely shocked when I opened up about my struggles. "But you always look so happy," they'd say, concerned and confused. I appreciated the compliment, but it only made me want to crawl back inside my castle and lock the door again. This approach was never intended to offend me, but it made me feel like my depression wasn't real. What I needed most in that time was for people to affirm my heartache, even if they couldn't see it. Other friends would try to fix my problems for me, immediately suggesting new tactics and techniques to feel joy. But at that time in my life, I didn't need solutions; I needed empathy. I appreciated the ideas, but I didn't have the energy to implement them. I just needed someone to sit with me in my sadness and acknowledge my pain. I needed people to commit to walking through the wilderness with me, instead of expecting me to heal overnight.

As I began to be more open about my mental health, some things in my life did change. I gradually accepted the truth that my sophomore year did not, in fact, live up to my impossible expectations. I got better at asking for help, prayer, and encouragement when I needed it most. I stopped crying in coffee shops and dreading my counseling sessions. But that doesn't mean the transition to authenticity was easy or simple.

when things
change
inside of
you, things
change
around you

I changed, and so did my friendships. Not every relationship of mine survived my blooming. I found that some of my people felt safer when I was acting as the isolated, masked version of me. But other friends gently grabbed my hand and stopped me from going back to my isolated, disingenuous, depressed ways. Over time my garden evolved into a healthier array of flowers.

When things change inside of you, things change around you. I've learned that change doesn't always mean growing apart; friends can also grow together. We can grow in the same direction, eventually blossoming into a unique bouquet, amplifying each other's beauty in contrast.

Mental health is difficult to talk about because, well, no one talks about it. But you can start. I know you are brave enough to tell the truth. You are strong enough to go first. Your conversations can stop the stigma. You never know if your story is the one somebody has been praying to hear.

11

Walking the Path

The process of healing is an endless zigzag. It's two steps forward and one step back, a million times over. It's often challenging to identify if you're actually making progress or if you're just walking around in circles where you've been stuck for months. I know, because I've been there. I've felt lost in the wilderness many times before.

Let's just get this out in the open: the path to healing is difficult and long and winding. It's far from cute or instantaneous. *Is healing worthwhile?* One hundred percent. *Is healing achievable?* Yes, with some help. *Does it happen overnight?* Rarely. I didn't feel automatically happy because I read a letter from my freshman self and invited a few friends into my struggle. I wasn't emotionally stable the moment I realized that my expectations were unrealistic and unhelpful. I didn't feel freedom from anxiety and depression after just one counseling session. Growing takes time.

To be completely "healed" isn't even really a destination we can get to. Sure, we can identify and restructure the broken parts of our lives one by one, achieving increasing peace with each reordering. But as imperfect human beings, we can always be reaching for a more fulfilling existence.

No matter how much progress we've made, we are always just a moment away from a situation that knocks us off our feet. Everything can change in an instant, potentially putting us right back where we started. So, rather than striving for ideal situations, our goal should be growth. Our aim should be physical, emotional, and spiritual balance. We should pursue wellness that allows us to healthily handle whatever life throws our way.

As second semester continued to unfold, I certainly experienced some "peak" moments along my path. I ran a half marathon, I fostered new relationships, and I enjoyed game nights with friends. I volunteered and laughed and read and explored and listened. There were some days so sweet and serendipitous that I forgot I'd ever been depressed.

But there were also the not-so-great days, the "valley" parts of my own unique path. There were many times I couldn't stop crying, times I was convinced I wasn't enough, and times I chose to isolate. There were days when I couldn't feel a thing and I'd overeat or overspend or overcommit in attempts to satisfy an endless chasm of loneliness.

As we dive into the stories in this chapter, I want to encourage you to toss your preconceived notions and your ten-step plan on "how to heal." Progress is a loop-de-loop, fluctuating journey with a general trend upward. Healing is a heart posture, not a list of habits. I want to offer my suggestions on the benefits of self-awareness, self-compassion, and self-love while understanding that there is no "one size fits all" way to grow.

* * *

healing is a heart posture

SELF-AWARENESS

Toward the end of my freshman year, I applied to be student leader for a church retreat the following fall. I can distinctly remember sitting in a coffee shop and completing the application. I had every question answered except for one. I stared at the blank spot on the application, completely baffled by what was being asked of me: "What are some of your strengths? What are some of your weaknesses? How do these qualities impact your leadership?"

Nineteen-year-old Victoria could not answer that seemingly simple question. At the time I could only identify my surface-level strengths and weaknesses. For example, I knew I was caring, generally organized, and pretty good at writing. I knew I was sometimes late and not very good at playing any sports involving a ball. But that was as deep as I got. It's crazy that we spend literally every moment of our lives with ourselves, and yet we still wonder who we truly are and what we truly want.

I carried that lack of self-awareness with me into my sophomore year, and then I fell into my slump. It's draining to live unaware of whom God made you to be. When we don't know who we are, we don't know what we need. Because I didn't understand the most basic of things about myself, like my strengths and weaknesses, I couldn't really identify that I was struggling until it was too late. Until I knew myself, I couldn't articulate my wants, needs, hopes, and fears. I think that it was only a matter of time before I crumbled under the weight of my uncertainty.

My healing expedition began with getting to know myself. I needed to understand who I was and what I wanted before I could design that life. Becoming self-aware is a lifelong trek through the wilderness. Especially for those with diagnosed mental health conditions, healing is a long-term process. The trek took much too long for my liking; I would have much rather sprinted down the path toward the finish line. But, as I've said before, healing doesn't happen overnight. It is in that steady stroll that we get to know who we truly are.

Throughout the rest of second semester, I often fell back into old habits and slipped into my anxiety and depression without even realizing it. But as I lived with the intention of self-awareness, I learned to pay attention to these things. I made the daily choice to check in on my own needs until it became a habit. I learned to monitor my progress.

Becoming self-aware didn't instantly put a stop to my self-destructive behavior or make my depression disappear. But as I made the conscious choices to think about my thinking and feel my feelings, I found more peace. I realized my journey didn't have to be a full-on sprint toward perfection; I just had to move forward one step at a time.

I moved forward by showing up at the counseling session even if I didn't want to. I moved forward by listening to the personal development podcasts instead of my self-deprecating thoughts. I moved forward by caring what God thought of me instead of obsessing over the opinions of others. I found healing in being present, seeking truth, and making brave choices. But I couldn't live in true emotional health until I overcame my inner critic.

SELF-COMPASSION

As I mentioned, healing can often feel like a step back instead of a step forward. As I became more self-aware with the help of counseling, introspection, journaling, and prayer, I began to analyze my beliefs and choices. I finally understood my strengths and weaknesses, but I criticized myself way more than I celebrated my strengths. Learning about my hidden brokenness felt like the complete opposite of progress.

The process of realizing my brokenness made me feel so much shame. I wanted to be someone without problems, but each counseling session illuminated yet another area of my life that needed fixing so that I could flourish. When my counselor gently pointed out my impossible expectations and inauthentic tendencies that sent me slumping, I interpreted her suggestions as attacks. I felt like my depression was my fault. I was so angry that I believed the lies that had led me to my sophomore slump.

One day during counseling, I learned something that changed my perspective on my past forever. I was talking about my previous beliefs and choices using harsh, self-defeating language.

I said, "I can't believe that I didn't know. I'm so dumb. My sadness is my fault. I should have never expected perfection like that. Life just isn't that good. I mess everything up. . . "

"Victoria," my counselor said, interrupting my shelf-shaming spiral. She looked at me with serious eyes. "You were doing the best you could with what you knew at the time. Give yourself grace. You can't change the past, so why make yourself feel bad about it?"

I stared blankly at the wall behind her. Her words were equal parts convicting and relieving.

"Have you heard the term self-compassion?" she asked.

I shook my head and listened to her explain the concept, a nonjudgmental approach to self-acceptance. Essentially, self-compassion is treating *yourself* the way you want to be treated—with dignity, kindness, acceptance, and grace.

Here's the truth: you can't change the past. Your decisions are permanent and your words have been said. You cannot go back in time and control your past self, but you can choose to reflect on your actions with compassion. You don't have to feel embarrassment or shame when you think about your past. At any moment you choose, you can embrace self-compassion over self-criticism.

It took me a while to understand self-compassion. Actually, it's something I really struggle with to this day. But when I'm feeling shame about my past beliefs and choices, I remember: "I was doing the best I could do with what I knew at the time."

SELF-LOVE

Let's recap here: self-awareness is necessary for healing, but it can lead to shame if we don't have compassion for our past selves. When I was first getting to know myself, I focused way too much on the negative aspects of my personality and lost my confidence. But self-compassion conquered my regrets. When I really started to give my past self grace, I saw my strengths instead of just my weaknesses. I realized that I could not change the past, so I might as well embrace it and learn from it. In that space of nonjudgmental acceptance, I found self-love.

Self-love is not arrogance or self-importance. Self-love is not pretending you are perfect (like I did at the start of my sophomore year) or denying where you need to grow. Self-love is simply understanding you are worthy of love and forgiveness right where you're at. It is seeing that, while you may be bruised, you are not permanently broken. Self-love is what will allow you to finally flourish. And you are very worthy of flourishing.

So, keep showing up. Show up when it feels natural and when it feels impossible. Show up with a smile or with tears on your face. Show up when you don't think you can. Show up when people don't understand. Be relentless in your pursuit of self-love.

* * *

While I was walking the path of healing as a second semester sophomore, something happened that only God could have planned. Something that reminded me that I was not alone—something that allowed me to feel true excitement, pride, and joy after not feeling anything for

99

months.

At the time, I was involved in the leadership of a campus organization for first-year students. This was the same leadership team that I told, "Today has been great, actually," after my coffee shop meltdown in the fall. As the year went on, I never explicitly the group them about my sophomore slump, although the opportunity arose many more times. Unfortunately, there were multiple team meetings that I entered after I'd been crying—with puffy eyes and splotchy cheeks to prove it.

In the spring, this campus leadership organization was in the process of planning an event to raise awareness for any cause of their choosing. As a member of the leadership team, I had the responsibility of facilitating a group of freshmen and helping them to plan and execute their chosen event. But before I could help with logistics, the freshmen needed to select a cause worth working for.

Every Tuesday night, I sat in the back of weekly cohort meetings and listened to freshmen debate which cause to support. They debated whether the event should strive to connect students, to promote academic integrity, or to encourage healthy lifestyle choices. They pondered whether we should work to help the campus or the community. They wanted to make an impact. Much to my surprise, the topic of "mental health advocacy" rose to top priority. As I listened to students share their experiences with stress, anxiety, and depression, I realized that these emotions were more common on campus than I once had thought. *Was everyone just that good at hiding their struggles? Or was I so self-consumed with my own striving to be perfect that I missed out on the greater picture?*

I'll never forget watching from the back of the room as the freshmen raised their hands in support of picking mental health as our cause. As I counted the anonymous vote, I felt shocked, confused, surprised, and comforted all at once. The cohort had just chosen to support my biggest struggle, and I was supposed to lead them through it. It was as if these freshmen knew exactly where I was struggling without me saying a word. God often works like that.

As the program directors announced that we would be supporting mental health, my stomach began to turn with anxiety. The other members of the leadership team were relieved the cohort had finally come to a consensus. I, on the other hand, was a jumble of emotion. *Was this a blessing or a disaster waiting to happen?* I wondered. *How could I advocate for something I haven't figured out for myself?*

I watched the cohort chat and celebrate as our meeting wrapped up. Standing alone in the back of the room, insecurity took me over. I didn't feel ready to lead this group. I didn't feel worthy of my position. I started to feel like this project was a personal attack—maybe everyone was onto me, maybe they knew about my depression and this was their way of exposing me. Maybe this situation was more of a cruel joke than it was a blessing. I wasn't ready to admit my deficiency. I wasn't ready to talk about mental health.

But, as God often does, He gave me what I didn't feel ready for in order to show me that He's the One doing the heavy lifting.

12

Light

Remember way back in the beginning of this book when I shared the story of admitting that my life didn't look exactly like I thought it would? Remember how earth-shattering and revolutionary that realization felt? Remember how foreign it was for me to accept that my life doesn't have to happen according to my timeline or match the expectations of others?

Well, to put things in perspective, that revelation happens around this part of the story, sometime in April of my sophomore year. My sophomore year had certainly not played out how I planned, and I finally realized there was nothing I could do to change the fact. April was when I started to come to terms with the "different." No more ignoring, minimizing, or justifying—just the slow process of acceptance.

As I adopted a more realistic view of my life, I became increasingly confident that I could someday find peace again. That day felt far, but at least I could see it now. I wasn't sure when and I wasn't sure how, but I believed I could live a life I loved. After accepting my struggle and admitting it to my close people, I decided it was time to take action. I was ready to stop ignoring my pain and to start minimizing the chances of slumping again.

With each counseling session, I learned that I was tied down by ropes of impossible expectations, black and white thinking patterns, the opinions of others, and self-doubt. Before admitting "my life doesn't look exactly like I thought it would," I just assumed I would have to live like that, bound and struggling forever. But after nine terrible months of battling the nasty voice inside of my head, I finally began to see the light.

For almost two years now, I've been in the process of untying the ropes that once hold me down. I want to unravel those gnarly old knots so I can finally fun free. I want to leave behind my past shame and sadness and step into a new life of peace, confidence, and joy. I believe God has already given me these gifts, but I often reject them in favor of worldly solutions like productivity and popularity. I'm slowly realizing that the things of this world won't untie my knots for me. I need to ask God for help and I need to trust the people and situations He puts in my life. The freedom is already there; I am the variable.

When I was in the depths of my anxiety and depression, my emotions controlled me completely. My emotions made me isolate, deny, overeat, and overcommit. My emotions held me as a prisoner of my own mind and convinced me of long, impossible narratives to explain the perfection I saw in everyone else. It made for a turbulent roller coaster of a life, with high highs and low lows and lots of crying.

At the start of second semester, my heart was so tired that I turned my emotions completely off. I was numb, not experiencing life to the fullest. It was in this back and forth, the drama and dullness, that I became completely disconnected from my own intuition. I stopped trusting myself.

I felt like I couldn't trust my emotions because they made me depressed. I didn't trust my numbness because it stole my joy. In April, I found myself not quite emotional and not quite numb—wanting to feel again but afraid of the consequences. I knew life had more to offer me. I wanted to trust, not fear, my feelings. I wanted back those instincts, passions, and perspectives that I used to posses.

Unfortunately, you can't just command yourself to "feel" and expect your brain and body to process everything in a healthy way. It took me a few months of unlearning and relearning to feel again. It's still a work in progress.

In counseling I realized that I held many untrue beliefs about emotions. I was conditioned to think that "good" emotions are praiseworthy and should be shared, while "negative" emotions should only be felt behind closed doors. I thought I was only valuable when I was cheerful and easy-going, so I saved my hard stuff for solitude. I wasn't actually processing my hurt, anger, and depression because I was scared of what it would do to the people I loved. I kept it all inside, wandering alone into the wilderness with only my dark feelings to keep me company. I didn't want to tell anyone how I was *really* doing, but in order to find healing, I'd have to open up. I'd have to listen to my emotions, share them with others, and learn to trust myself again.

I used to think that being diagnosed with depression meant I was broken. I believed that God gave me messed-up emotions that couldn't be trusted. I used to be a victim of my sadness, and so when I felt depressed, I'd give up and give in. I was bossed around by my brain. I had no agency in my life—I either felt overly emotional or nothing at all. But it's not supposed to be that way.

I remember one particularly vulnerable conversation with a friend when I said, "How am I supposed to trust my emotions? I never know if they are from me or my depression."

She looked me in the eyes and said, "Your feelings are telling you something important, even the sad ones. Your emotions are trustworthy because they're yours. But you get to decide how to respond to those emotions."

I wish I could look you in the eye and say the same thing.

your feelings do not change your ability to be loved

I used to believe that I was "lovable" or "bearable" or "easy to be around" only when I was happy. I thought I was "difficult" or "draining" or "annoying" when I was sad. But these beliefs are not realistic or healthy. Feelings do not deserve value judgements, and neither do you. Your worth doesn't change based on your emotional state. Your feelings do not change your ability to be loved. You've lived too long in denial and distrust. It's time to acknowledge your emotions without letting them control you. You can respect your feelings without acting on them. It is time to trust yourself.

I once heard a pastor compare negative emotions to the warning lights on the dashboard of a car. The warning symbols illuminate when something is wrong. If you drive around for miles and miles with the warning lights on, you'll eventually break down. At some point, your choice to ignore the warning signs will hurt you. The damage to your vehicle could be catastrophic. It could be expensive, time consuming, and even dangerous. When you ignore those warning lights, you create a big problem for yourself in the future. The same is true for emotions. When you feel something uncomfortable, it's worth acknowledging in the moment; otherwise, you're bound to break down in the future.

I used to view my negative emotions (warning lights) as unworthy of attention. I ignored all of my uncomfortable feelings, and after a few months my metaphorical dashboard was lit up with warnings like a Christmas tree. Mix in a busy schedule (my car was going full speed first semester) and an insistence on never showing those warning lights to a mechanic, and you're going to crash.

When I look at things this way, I understand why I broke down in the fall. I waited far too long to address my "warning lights," and so I exploded in anxiety and depression. Once my car finally stopped moving and I had enough time to assess the situation, I vowed to never feel again. And that's how I found myself disconnected from my emotions.

Your feelings, even the uncomfortable ones, are worth addressing. Emotions are not meant to control us, but they are meant to be felt. There's always a deeper meaning behind difficult feelings, like stress or anxiety or sadness. They aren't pleasant, but you didn't do anything wrong to have them. Those feelings are valid because they're yours. But just because emotions are always valid, that doesn't mean they are always true.

The more I think about it, the more I believe that we were *created* to feel the entire spectrum of emotions.

Confusion.

Guilt.

Grief.

Hesitation.

Feeling excluded.

Feeling included.

Creativity.

Hope.

Gratitude.

Belonging.

While my first instinct is often to run from pain and deny my hurt, I now know the difference between my emotions *feeling* bad to experience and my emotions *making* me a bad human being. My worth doesn't change when I'm happy or sad. Your worth doesn't change either. No matter if you're feeling abandoned, embarrassed, disapproving, skeptical, infuriated, aggressive, or nervous, you are still worthy.

You're worthy of a life you love.

You are worthy of confidence and security.

You're worthy of more than depression and anxiety.

You're worthy of a life that isn't just numb.

You're worthy of friends who will accept you in every emotional state.

107

You're worthy of accepting *yourself* in every emotional state.

I used to ignore my uncomfortable feelings. I exhausted myself by forcing fake joy. I thought this was the way to happiness, but I couldn't have been more wrong. Now, I understand that all feelings are worthy of being felt. I know that my feelings do not have to shake my faith. I believe that God has good plans for my life, and I think my feelings are one of the many things God is using to point me toward those plans.

Instead of ignoring your warning lights, I'd encourage you to try this: feel it, name it, and move forward. Allow yourself to be honest. Stop letting the sensation of your emotion define your worth. Feel it. Name it. Move forward. This may feel reckless at first, but I promise the process is teaching you something. Oftentimes, the consequence of lashing out, hanging up, or going silent are much greater than the reward. Over time you will learn that all feelings should be felt, but not all feelings should be acted on.

In the uncomfortable space between what you *want to do* and what you know is right, you will find your principles. This is where concepts like grace, selflessness, justice, advocacy, and acceptance come in. These are not unconscious feelings, but rather, conscious agents in our decisions. These principles will guide you as you move forward.

Feel your feelings. Act on your principles.

This process slowly built up my confidence. As I made the conscious choice to feel my feelings and act on my principles, I learned to trust my emotions again.

* * *

As the spring continued to unfold, I was repeatedly surprised by my external circumstances. God knew that I needed every possible reminder that life could be enjoyable after a dark season. These little glimpses of happiness encouraged me that the hard work of healing was worth my pursuit. Life wasn't what I expected, but it was still good. The spring of sophomore year began the my long process of accepting that "different" does not always mean "worse."

One of the most life-giving parts of my sophomore spring was leading the student organization that had chosen to support mental health. With each weekly meeting, the freshmen cohort clarified the event and its goals. We decided to host a campus walk/run celebration to raise money for the American Foundation for Suicide Prevention. We would call it "Mental Health Mile." There would be music, a food truck, and a raffle. The event would happen at sunset, and we would all wear yellow shirts and glow sticks to remind students to "be the light."

I think God intentionally put me on the leadership of that organization knowing full well how much it would bless me to advocate and fundraise for something I personally struggled with. While I was technically tasked with leading the cohort, I was learning just as much as they were. As we prepared for the event, I heard more about the mental health battles that college students fought daily. We created an environment where mental health was an acceptable topic of conversation. I heard stories of homesickness, stress, and comparison on social media, which were all things I'd struggled with but never had opened up about. I was shocked to hear the struggles of people I'd perceived as "perfect." As I listened, it became increasingly clear that not everyone has a diagnosed mental illness, but every single person has mental health they must fight to preserve. My depression had convinced me that I was the only one struggling, but that was far from the truth.

* * *

Depression has a way of making the world feel so small. It locks you in your own little box, isolated from everyone else. Darkness is all you know, and darkness is all you think you're worthy of. You're stuck in the shadows of your own brain. If you stay boxed in for too long, you'll stop believing that life has anything more to offer you. You'll forget about the light you used to see.

Until by God's grace, a tiny sliver of sunshine seeps in through the cracks. The light reminds you how things used to be, back when you lived free from the constraints of depression. For a moment you are free from the anxiety and overthinking and people-pleasing and insecurity that boxed you in. The light has conquered the dark.

Some may find this light in a laugh, a sunrise, or a home-cooked meal. For others it might be found in a movie, a song, or a quote. You may find this light in a friend, a counselor, a parent, or a group of people. The light could be in a bouquet of flowers, the undeserved kindness of a stranger, a newborn baby, or a good night's sleep. The light shines in endless forms.

The light reminds you that life outside of your box is, and has always been, bright and brilliant. You were not made to stay in the shadows forever, even if isolation is more comfortable than vulnerability. The light you see is not guaranteed to be safe; it may very well leave you squinting and sunburned. But something about it draws you in. Your heart knows that freedom is worth the risk.

Someday this light will show up in your life. I'm sure of it. Soon you will see outside of your box and realize there is more goodness happening in the world than the sadness happening inside of your head. Once you see the light, you'll search for it everywhere—the chase is addicting. You'll begin finding joy in the things you once took for granted. You will begin living in pursuit of light. You will be inspired by the mundane. You will be more grateful. As you look for the light, you'll begin to believe in the goodness of life, the kindness of humanity, and the love of God once again. The light will destroy your darkness bit by bit until, eventually, it is bright enough for you to see again.

The box may not be gone, but it is no longer dark inside.

Depression may still be there, but it cannot steal your joy.

13

Peace

Everyone is fighting a battle you know nothing about, even your closest family members and friends. While you may know them deeply, you do not live inside their brains. You do not hear the constant stream of thoughts flowing through their heads. The only mind you can truly know is your own.

I feel like we've spent a lot of this book together focusing on ourselves. As I've shared the story of my sophomore year, we've learned about escapism, vulnerability, emotions, and expectations. I hope and pray that these chapters have encouraged you to evaluate your own mental health and happiness. But what about everyone else in your life?

The process of healing can unintentionally become a bit self-centered. I know because I've been there. When personal happiness and health is the goal, it's easy to forget about others in the process. In the past I've ignored other's needs in favor of meeting my own. I've prioritized my healing over my service to others, which is why I want to repeat myself here: everyone is fighting a battle you know nothing about. We can't spend all of our energy fixing ourselves; we must also check in on others.

One of my favorite quotes is "You can't pour from an empty cup," meaning, "You can't give to others what you haven't given yourself." I believe that this is true, but sometimes its presentation is a bit misconstrued. Too often we focus on only the filling, thanks to the current cultural emphasis on self-care. But I think we should focus on two separate, uniquely important parts of this statement: the pouring out *and* the filling up.

POURING OUT

At the start of sophomore year, all my focus was always on "pouring out." I put all my energy into ensuring that the people around me were taken care of. I wanted to be known for being able to help at all times, so I said "yes" to obligations that were never meant for me.

I remember one morning in September when I woke up feeling absolutely obliterated by my schedule. I was exhausted from the busy day before and a restless night of sleep. I had another jam-packed agenda in front of me with no room to reschedule. My life was overwhelming me, but I felt stuck. I had signed up for all of this. *Shouldn't I be grateful for these opportunities? What would people think of me if I cancelled?* I looked at my phone with a dozen texts awaiting my response and then opened my paper planner to see back-to-back meetings. I wanted to give, but I had nothing left. I was running on empty.

I remember praying desperately, asking God to give me what I needed to get through the day. I asked for enough energy to love all people and enough time to be there for everyone. I requested boundless love and stretched time from God, but these are gifts only God is powerful enough to possess. Even when my body was in desperate need of a break, my focus was never on filling up. I just poured and poured until my cup was completely empty. Now I understand that it is not my job to meet everyone's needs. After all, if I could meet everyone's needs, why would they need to trust in God?

When I was feeling worn out during my sophomore year, I thought that I was the problem. I thought that I just needed more energy or time or passion or capacity. But looking back, I see that what I really needed was a different schedule. As I reflect on my "pouring out," I can understand why I eventually got so sick and tired of my own life. I was pouring and pouring and pouring until I ran out of love to give. I was trying to be everything to everyone. I was playing a role I was never supposed to play, taking on a job that was never meant to be mine.

FILLING UP

It wasn't long before my sophomore self was completely spent from the constant "pouring out." I felt like I had simply nothing to give, and even the smallest tasks seemed impossibly overwhelming. At some point my depression forced me to stop pouring. I literally did not have the energy for relationships, participation, favors, and kindness. At the time my lack made me feel like a failure, but when I look back, I realize that I was just trying to pour from an empty cup.

As exhausting as it was to try and fill everyone else's cups, I liked the validation it used to give me. I loved when people told me "Thank you" or "I couldn't do it without you." Back then, I thought my value came from how I could help people and not from who I am. I didn't think I was lovable without my favors.

After a few counseling sessions, I realized my cup was totally empty. So, I decided to focus solely on filling back up. My goal was not to change any part of my lifestyle long term; I just wanted to get back to being helpful and appreciated. I wanted to recharge and then return to my old people-pleasing ways. I worried my friends would leave me now that I didn't have anything to give or provide for them. So, I made every effort to fill up my own cup with the intention of eventually pouring it all back out.

I had never really intentionally taken care of myself before then, but once I started, I couldn't stop. Self-indulgence was too comfortable. After years of neglecting my needs, I binged on self-care. Filling my cup was so much easier than sacrificing for others. So, for a few months, I forgot about the importance of pouring out.

After a few months of extreme inward focus, my cup was full again. I had enough to share with others, but this time, I refused to do so. I was afraid of loving people again after my generosity had hurt me in the past. I was secure, but I was being selfish. I was holding onto a fullness that was meant to be shared.

GLASS HALF FULL

To be honest, I didn't realize that I was living life with a "full cup" until recently. I spent months filling back up before I realized how self-centered I'd become in the process of healing. I was filling my cup in order to please myself rather than to serve others. In both cases, the outcome is the same—the cup is full. But the intention is vastly different based on what you plan to do with this "fullness." Did you fill up to serve others, or are you hoarding your happiness?

Instead of living completely full or completely empty, I believe that we should live with our glasses half full. That way, we have both the supply to pour out and the space to be filled. Again, like black and white thinking, life does not have to be completely one thing or the other. We have more options than just "full" or "empty." We can give and receive. We can love and be loved. This is the life we were created for.

I grew up giving and giving and giving until my source eventually ran dry. During my sophomore year I was tired, empty, and depressed. Then I took and took and took, and the taking felt so safe that I never gave anything away. I accidentally became self-centered and stubborn.

115

These days, I'm trying to find the appropriate volume to keep in my cup at all times. Instead of being a martyr with an empty cup or a hermit with a full one, I'm striving to find the healthy space between. I don't want to be so full that I forget my weakness, but I don't want to be so empty that I run out of strength. I think we all deserve both the opportunity to give and to take.

As I write about this topic, part of me wishes that I'd always known about this balance between pouring out and filling up. Sometimes I wonder what I would be like if I had skipped both my depletion phase and my binge. But I can't change the past, and I refuse to shame myself for it. I learned a lot from both my times of emptiness and overflow, so I will choose to be grateful and will let it be, moving forward with my glass half full.

As I learn to live with my "glass half full," I must be intentional about what I am doing to fill up *and* what I am doing to pour out. Both actions matter; it is not one or the other. In order to live with intention, we must do a bit of introspection and planning.

My counselor told me to make a list of ways to fill up and ways I want to pour out. I thought about it for a few weeks and here's what I got:

Filling Up:

- A morning run while listening to new music
- Sipping hot black coffee while doing Bible study
- Getting seven or eight hours of sleep each night
- Choosing healthy foods that bless my body
- Reading books and listening to podcasts that inspire me

Pouring Out:

- Mentoring young women as they grow in their faith
- Volunteering with the children's ministry at my church
- Writing blog posts and emails that encourage others
- Doing random acts of kindness when a friend has a rough day
- Making time to connect with my family from miles away

These are just a few ideas that may inspire you along your journey of "living half full." It's taken me some time to find the things that make me feel truly rested and excited to serve. I don't want to fill up and pour out in a certain way just because it's what I think I *should* be doing or what the world tells me is the "right" thing; I want to make choices that honor my needs and desires. I want to pour out and be poured into in ways that feel authentic and realistic.

I've also learned that every person has different needs and different passions. So, your list may look very different than mine. That should not be a cause for comparison but rather, a cause for celebration. Our different preferences of recharging and contributing are crucial to ensuring that everyone is taken care of. There's no rulebook to live with your cup half full. Anyone who tells you differently is neglecting to see the beauty that comes with diversity.

* * *

As you make a conscious effort to "pour out" you may find an act of service that feels natural to you. It doesn't feel like a burden or chore. It doesn't mean this activity comes without sacrifice, but it brings you real, authentic joy. For me this kind of service comes in the form of mentorship. I love taking care of people who are a few steps behind me in life. I love reaching back, grabbing their hands, and guiding them through the places I've recently walked. When I was in high school, these people were my younger friends at dance. In college I've found a handful of these people to love and serve, not just for the sake of their younger age but for the ways they teach and inspire me daily. Building relationships with younger people isn't just an activity to put on my resume. It is something that my heart needs to thrive. This is the kind of service you should prioritize—the things that make you feel the most "yourself."

I found quite a few of these younger friends in that freshman leadership organization I've mentioned before. I think this is part of the reason why I was so greatly impacted by the freshman cohort's choice to advocate for mental health with their Mental Health Mile. Through March, April, and May, I helped the cohort work tirelessly to prepare for the big event. I was consistently blown away by their fierce dedication to a cause that impacted me much more than I let on.

As we planned, I continued to keep my mental health struggles a secret. I was still so ashamed of my sophomore slump. One evening in a leadership meeting, we discussed the cohorts' idea to make meal buttons for Mental Health Mile participants to wear. The bright yellow buttons would read, "I run for _," so that event participants could fill in the blank with a name of someone who struggles with mental health and wear the button as a sign of support and solidarity. I hated this idea.

As we discussed the possibility of buttons, I stayed quiet. If the buttons were for any other cause, I would have joined my fellow leadership team members in their affirming nods and excitement. But this felt too personal, like the idea was planned to expose my weakness. My mind began to race with worry.

I didn't want my name in the button's blank. I hated the fact that I'd struggled enough to be put in the category of "mentally ill." I had no confidence in my story, my struggle, or my strength. I felt broken, like

118

it was more difficult to be a human for me than it was for anyone else. I anxiously chewed my nails for the rest of the meeting and wondered whose name I'd write on my button at the event.

* * *

A few weeks later, a couple hundred students, community members, and university faculty gathered in the campus commons at sunset for the Mental Health Mile. The whole evening felt surreal; I felt so proud as I watched the cohort's dedication unfold into a beautiful celebration of light and truth. The Mental Health Mile brought triumph to a topic so rarely talked about.

Even as I answered questions and facilitated the event wearing a Mental Health Mile T-shirt, I felt like a victim instead of an advocate. I didn't feel equipped to lead these freshmen because of my own mental health secrets. I feared the cohort would stop loving me or trusting me once they found out about my diagnosis. This event felt like the perfect place for my weakness to show. Heart racing and palms sweaty, I stayed busy working the raffle table to avoid writing a name on one of those dreaded "I run for _" buttons.

After a half hour of mingling, the event participants began the race around campus in their bright yellow shirts and shining glow sticks while I stayed back. I watched the group begin their mile loop, tiny yellow blurs of being getting smaller with each step. I hoped the cohort was enjoying the event they'd planned so successfully. They cheered and sang and danced and laughed, glow stick necklaces bobbing in the evening dusk. I felt anxious and uptight as I surveyed the sea of smiling people. *Why couldn't I just be happy like everyone else? Why were my emotions so complicated and isolating?*

In the suddenly empty campus commons, I watched the sky change from a clear blue to a soft swirl of orange and pink. It was the first time in a long time that I was truly still, without occupation or obligation to distract me. Without the leadership responsibilities to keep me busy, I relaxed into the present moment. Staring off into the sunset, I couldn't help but replay mental memories of my sophomore year.

Driving from Colorado to Texas, confident for all the wrong reasons.

Moving into the sorority house, unpacking my impossible expectations.

Nonstop days of classes and meetings and to-dos. Trying to be it all.

Sleepless, sweat-soaked nights.

Crying in cars, sorority house showers, coffee shops.

A note from a stranger. The trash can. A text.

Losing my love for my life. Feeling overwhelmed by my commitments and betrayed by my anxious mind.

An unrelenting stomach ache and sweaty hands.

A very empty cup.

The gray.

A brief interjection of bright light; two words at a dining hall.

"Me too."

Counseling.

An anxiety attack on the beach.

Posting falsified perfection. Refreshing the screen to be virtually validated.

Drastic external change. Internal ignorance.

Counseling.

Being honest with myself.

Being honest with my people.

Counseling.

Self-awareness. Self-compassion. Self-love.

Trust.

Peace.

As I came back to reality after my mental montage, I experienced a peace more real than my darkest feelings. I felt a stillness, a calmness, a contentment. For once my anxious heart slowed its flutter, and I melted into the present moment: leading people I loved, supporting a cause I was passionate about, and pouring out and filling up at the same time.

I noticed my feet on the campus of my dream school, the calming trickle of a landmark fountain, and the feeling of a soft Texas breeze dancing through my hair. I saw the first tiny stars peeking out behind a darkening curtain of sky. I took a deep breath and felt that I was not alone. In that moment I believed my life had purpose and value, even if I couldn't explain it. I felt a tiny flicker of confidence; a light inside me, aching to glow.

I looked down at my yellow T-shirt and read the words on the front. *"Be the Light."*

Before I even realized what I was doing, my legs began moving instinctually, effortlessly, as if this were the moment I was made for. I walked over to the table with the "I run for _" buttons scattered across an orange table cloth. I grabbed the cool, yellow metal of a blank button and a black marker. With a deep breath I cautiously filled in the blank: "I run for *myself.*"

Peace.

you are never alone in your suffering

Epilogue

"You do not have to live afraid. You do not have to live in an overgrown garden of weeds that have no place." —*Morgan Harper Nichols* [2]

I recently switched counselors, not because there was a problem but simply because of a change in circumstances. My first counselor, the one who faithfully left me voicemails back when I was too afraid to admit my struggle, recently decided to pause her practice for a while so that she could spend more time with her daughter. I really respect her decision, and I'm not sure it's one I would be strong enough to make. She did what was best for her, even when others were counting on her. She trusted God to take care of the people she cares about.

When I first heard the news that she wouldn't be offering counseling services anymore, I was disappointed and a little angry. After knowing her for more than a year, I finally felt comfortable to be my most authentic self with her. She knew the names of my family and friends. She knew the backstory behind almost every situation, and she always had the right follow-up questions to ask. I finally had stopped dreading counseling sessions and had begun to see them as opportunities to grow. But now, I'd have to repeat the entire awkward process with someone new.

The transition to a new counselor over the past few months has been smoother than I expected. Although I am meeting with a different person, counseling is still very helpful. I wouldn't currently classify myself as deeply struggling, but it is healthy for me to have a safe space to verbally process my life. I'm not sure that I'll be in counseling forever, but it's working for now so I will continue until it feels safe and healthy to take a break.

While I've had an overall positive experience with the new counselor, I'd be lying if I told you that I've never wished I could go back to my first. There are moments when I wish I could return to what was so comfortable. But, if I've learned anything lately, it's that we cannot grow unless we get uncomfortable every once and awhile. So, I am showing up with my full self, even in the awkwardness. I am trusting in God's plan, even when my life doesn't look like I thought it would.

A few days ago, I was meeting with my new counselor when she said something deeply impactful to me and relevant to this book. She had no idea my book was full of metaphors about gardens, weeds, and flowers, but that's the illustration she chose to demonstrate an important truth.

"Imagine that all the difficult parts of your life—your anxiety, depression, and insecurity—are like weeds in a garden," she said.

I nodded, laughing internally. It was as if she knew I was in the process of finishing this book, in search of one final metaphor to wrap things up.

She continued, "If you just focus on pulling up all the weeds, what will your garden look like?"

I thought for a second, afraid I would answer incorrectly. Hesitantly, I replied, "I guess the garden would just be really empty. There would probably be grass, no flowers?"

"Yep, that's right," she responded calmly. "There won't be much of anything growing there. So, what do you think is more beautiful: an empty garden or a full one?"

"Um, I guess an empty garden isn't as beautiful as it could be," I said, slowly beginning to understand where she was going with this metaphor.

My new counselor nodded and said, "So, what are you going to plant where the weeds used to be?"

I paused deep in thought. I'd never considered the importance of planting new flowers because I'd always been so obsessed with pulling up old weeds. I wanted the anxiety, depression, and insecurity to be gone, but I never thought about what I wanted to grow in their place. I stared off into space for a few moments before she continued.

She said, "I think sometimes, when people are healing from hurt, rejection, disappointment, or depression, they become so focused on getting rid of those wounds that they forget about the other parts of their lives."

The new counselor had just hit me with the truth of my own story. It was crazy how she knew me so well after only a few sessions. For a moment, everything felt right. I knew that God had matched me with this counselor at this time for a reason.

She continued, "You can spend the rest of your life obsessed with removing the negative things. But think about how your life will look once they're all finally gone. You don't want to live an empty life."

I nodded, slowly coming to terms with the truth. She was describing to me exactly what I'd been doing for the past year.

She said, "Or you can try to plant beautiful things where the weeds used to be. You pull out those weeds either way, but your garden looks very different based on what you do with the new open space. So, are you going to leave your garden barren and dry, or are you going to plant new life where the weeds used to be?"

I want to leave you with the same question: are you going to obsess over your weeding and leave your garden empty? Or will you give something new the opportunity to grow?

An empty life is not as fulfilling as it could be. Sure, empty is safe, predictable, and secure. But a barren garden is not nearly as beautiful as a garden that is flourishing and filled with a variety of colorful life—a curated little ecosystem actively growing every day. Gardens are meant to be filled with flowers, and human lives are meant to grow bravery and authenticity and courage and confidence. A life that grows these things is never guaranteed to be simple or unchallenging. But this way is always worth it.

You've got one life, one garden, to weed and to plant. You control what you reap and what you sow. You can let the weeds take you over, you can choose nothingness over beauty, or you can take the risk of planting and tending to the things that matter most:

Relationships.

Passions.

Dreams.

Beliefs.

Hobbies.

Service.

Sacrifice.

Love.

These things aren't always simple. Gardens require consistent attention and care. But the way I see it, life on this earth will be inevitably unpredictable, stretching, and hard. If I can't control what happens to me, I want to control how I respond. I don't want to sit around all alone in a dusty, empty garden, afraid of danger and change that I really can't control. I want to enjoy the beauty of friendships and hobbies and passions and dreams while I have them. I want my garden to inspire and motivate others.

Your life is too short and too precious to spend living in fear. You are worthy of a life that shocks you with its wild beauty and spontaneous blooms. You deserve more than emptiness and isolation. You deserve more than depression and anxiety. You deserve a life you love to live. You deserve purpose. You deserve progress. You deserve peace.

Acknowledgments

Writing this book has been a true testament to God's power and faithfulness. As a sophomore I never imagined He'd use my story in this way. Over the past few months of writing, I've been able to see how He was always orchestrating my life to bring Him glory. With God in control, no moment is ever wasted.

To My Family: I wouldn't have written this book without your unconditional love and support. Thank you for filling me with the confidence I needed to chase this dream.

To My Sister, Lizzie: You are a breath of fresh air. Thank you for accepting me just the way I am while also inspiring me to be more educated and inclusive. You help me to see the world in new ways.

Elle: Thank you for encouraging me to start a blog that one rainy evening in December. You have an incredible gift to see the potential in others before they see it in themselves. You are my forever best friend.

Blake: Knowing you is one of the biggest blessings of college. The way you believe in people is life-changing and I am honored to be on the receiving end of your support. (And thank you for the incredible cover art! You are so gifted.)

Chandler: Time with you makes me feel safe, loved, and capable. Thank you for listening to my feelings over TJ's pumpkin spice coffee and never making me feel crazy or alone.

To My First Draft Readers: Thank you for having the eyes to catch my typos and the hearts to support my dreams. I know you spent lots of time reading my messy first drafts, and I am so grateful.

Katrina: You've seen this project from the very beginning, and you've never stopped cheering me on. I am so thankful for a friend like you.

Iris: Thank you for staying so faithfully invested in my life for all these years. You celebrate people exactly as they are, and that is so powerful. I could not love you more!

Lauren L.: You teach me so much about Jesus and I am honored to do life with you. I am so proud of you and I know God is using your story in big ways.

Julia Q.: I am so thankful that I sat next to you on that flight home for winter break. Thank you for being so genuinely excited about this book and for showing me what it looks like to trust God in all seasons.

Julia G.: Thank you for loving me through the highs and lows of college—I am so grateful that God put us in the same dorm during our freshman year.

Hanna: You make me feel so comfortable being myself. Thank you for being so inclusive, honest, and encouraging, always. You are a true friend.

Kathryn: Thank you for being so attentive and involved in my book writing process. You have taught me so much.

To all those who celebrated me, cared for me, listened to me, laughed with me, cried with me, and supported me along this journey—thank you. Thank you for believing in a book you hadn't even read. I do not say this lightly: I could not have done this without you.

To Jesus: You are the way in the wilderness.

Notes

OASIS

1   "Escapism." *Merriam-Webster.com Dictionary*, Merriam-Webster, https://www.merriam-webster.com/dictionary/escapism. Accessed 24 Sep. 2020.

EPILOGUE

2   "For the Mind." *All Along You Were Blooming: Thoughts for Boundless Living*, by Morgan Harper Nichols, Zondervan, 2020, pp. 68.

About the Author

Victoria Becker is fascinated by words and passionate about people. Originally from Denver, Colorado, Victoria is uncertain of where she's headed next, but she's confident in God's plans for the future. *A Way in the Wilderness* is her first book and she hopes to write many more. Connect with her at victorialisa.com or @words.vlb on Instagram.

CPSIA information can be obtained
at www.ICGtesting.com
Printed in the USA
LVHW031359121120
671523LV00039B/1208